JOE SEMLER
PLAYING BASEBALL
IN THE 1920's & 30'S

BY

Edward Leo Semler Jr.

Copyright © 2020 by Edward Leo Semler Jr.

All rights reserved by the author.

First Edition: 2020

Library of Congress Control Number: 2020920433

ISBN: 978-0-578-76473-3

Printed in the United States of America

City of Publication; Schulenburg, Texas

Cover layout by Edward Leo Semler Jr.

To the family of Joseph F. Semler and those who love baseball

TABLE OF CONTENTS

Introduction	1
The Early Years 1919 to 1922	7
Beaver Falls Elks & Bellevue 1922 to 1928	25
Homewood-Brushton 1929 to 1930	99
Hazleton Mountaineers 1931 to 1932	127
Scranton Miners 1932	161
York White Roses 1932	165
Wilkes-Barre Barons 1933 to 1934	171
Nashville Volunteers 1935	199
Wilkes-Barre Barons 1935 to 1936	209
The Late Years 1937 to 1940's	235

Minor League Stats	243
Resources	245
About The Author	249

Introduction

I'm a little out of my element writing about baseball, although I have played it off and on most of my life to include adult baseball. My previous six books have been about the military and military related history. But I'm really excited to get out of my normal writing genre to write about my grandfather's baseball career, predominantly in the 1920's and 30's, when baseball produced arguably some of its best players ever. Guys like Babe Ruth, Joe Dimaggio, and Lou Gehrig in the Major Leagues, Satchel Paige, Josh Gibson, and Cool Papa Bell in the Negro Leagues.

But back in the 1920's and 30's, like now, those great players filtered through the semi-pro and the minor leagues on their way to the major league, except for the Negro League players who played up into the minors until desegregation of baseball. Reaching the major leagues was the goal, or so I thought. Because back in the 1920's and 30's a minor league baseball player could make more money than playing in the major leagues. And minor league teams were a little more popular in some areas of the country because there were no major league teams nearby.

My dad once asked my grandfather, Joe Semler, why he never played in the major leagues. He told him he that he was offered several contracts by the Cincinnati Reds but he was making just as much money in the semi-pros at the time. He said in hindsight it was a mistake to have turned down the offers, because he never played in the major leagues.[47]

That's a luxury I had with my grandfather, I knew him well into my teens and had sat around and listened to his baseball stories. Baseball was always a part of his life and he kept up with it in the newspaper and on the radio. A common way to greet him was to ask him "how did the Pirates do yesterday." And he would tell you anything you wanted to know about the game down to how many hits any one player had.

He was an interesting man and usually talking about baseball when he was sitting on the front porch enjoying his swing and spitting his leaf tobacco into a coffee can. That is as long as the Pirates weren't on the radio! Then there was to be no chatter, just listening to the announcer give the play by play of the game.

Joe, as I will refer to him from now on, would more or less rock than swing, with his feet firmly placed on the ground. He would lean forward, sort of hunched over, rubbing his huge worn hands together, which looked like leather, while he talked or listened to the radio. On a forward rock he would let loose with a big spit towards the coffee can off to the corner, usually hitting it. In the colder months you would find him in the kitchen sitting pretty much the same way. The leaf tobacco would be replaced with a cigarette and he would pass the time dipping a piece of bread covered in butter and jelly, that he would fold in half and dunk into his coffee, which was pretty much milk and sugar with a splash of coffee.

And when any of my cousins or I would ask him a question about baseball we of course wanted to know if he had ever played for the Pittsburgh Pirates or stuck out anyone famous like Babe Ruth! Because the Pirates and Babe Ruth were as big as you could get as far as we knew.

Joe was as a relatively big man for the times at almost 6 feet tall and 170 pounds of German stock. He was referred to by team mates as simply "Joe." But he did have nicknames such as "Smoky Joe" because of his fastball, "Big Joe", and "Josey." He enjoyed playing baseball but it wasn't his livelihood. He was a carpenter by trade and that's where he drew most of his income. He played baseball during the season, which was April through September, which was added income. When he played semi-pro ball, the games were held on the weekends or evenings during the week. This allowed players to maintain their regular jobs. Once he was playing in the minor league's baseball became a full-time job and his lively hood during the baseball season because it was so much more demanding and required a lot of traveling. But he would still return to his carpentry and family-owned construction business in the off season.

Whenever I would make a trip into Pittsburgh with my dad, he would constantly be pointing out buildings that were built by his father, Joe, and their family business. Even after moving out to the suburbs of Allison Park in the 50's Joe continued on as a builder and farmer. When I went to buy a new truck after being discharged from the Army in 1985, I went to nearby Tom Henry Chevrolet. It's a big dealership along Route 8 in Allison Park. As I was filling out the paperwork the salesman recognized my name and asked me if I was related to Joe Semler. When I replied that he was my grandfather the salesman said that Joe had built this building that we were sitting in, and we both stopped and took a minute to let our eyes soak up the interior. Obviously happy with Joe's work the salesman told me he was giving me 10% off my truck!

And that's the impression he left on people. In researching this book it's a constant in the newspaper articles written about him - how he was a *"real gentleman."*[1] And fellow teammate Dr. Richard "Dick" Goldberg said years after playing with Joe that *"He couldn't recall any one pitcher in our heyday that was better than big Joe. We were teammates on the Beaver Falls Elks, as well as many other teams around Pittsburgh and Ohio towns. What a pitcher, and what a personality! In all the years I've known Joe, I've never seen him lose his temper."*[2] But I didn't need to read it to know it, I knew the man and personally experienced how good of a person he was.

My biggest regret in writing this book is that I didn't write it when Joe was still alive. It would have helped in closing the loop on some back stories, I'm sure. But there was so much written about him in newspaper articles that I feel the story is told appropriately.

Joe passed away in 1980 at the age of 80. Born in 1899 he had lived a full life. I have many fond memories of him and vividly remember him the last time I saw him. My dad was being assigned to Australia in 1979 for several years with the government and we visited with Joe before leaving. He wasn't in the best shape health wise, but I didn't even consider the fact that he wouldn't be there when we got back. We hadn't been in Australia long when he passed away and my dad flew back home alone for the funeral. Joe is buried just a mile or so from where he grew up on Graydan Avenue in McKees Rocks where he spent most of his life, and played a majority of his baseball.

This book was challenging to put together because I really didn't know how much information I was going to be able to find on Joe's playing career. I had actually thought about putting it together several times over the years but it never took off. But now with newspapers being digitalized and easily accessible I picked the project up again. Once I started to go through newspaper archives, I found that his career was in fact well documented. Of course, when he first started to play in 1919 news coverage was limited in quantity and description. But as he became more popular and played on better teams, he received better coverage and his career became more detailed. This in itself became an issue for me as I tried to figure out exactly how I was going to present this to the reader. I eventually decided to just write about every game Joe played in that I came across, because I think they give you a feel of the ups and downs that is baseball. If I just wrote about Joes good games you would walk away from this book thinking Joe had a perfect career with a bunch of wins. But there were good games and bad games. And I think it really captures baseball in the roaring 20's and depressed 30's and how it was so important to everyone at the time as a national pastime.

I also have to apologize for the quality of the pictures in the printed version of this book. The majority of these are from newspapers that were of a very poor quality to begin with. They also liked to run their pictures the width of the newspaper which at the time was great for the reader. But trying to condense that picture onto an area a ¼ of that size isn't practical. The pictures in the eBook version are much easier to view because you can enlarge and zoom in on them. But have no fear because I have referenced every picture so you can easily go and find it in the newspaper that it was printed in and view it as it was originally presented. I also tried to include the date of every game I talk about so if you would like to read more about it you can easily reference it in a newspaper search query.

I have also laid the book out in chronological order of his playing years so you can easily flip to a team he played for. Because this book isn't a biography of Joe's life, but a detailing of his playing career, you can easily jump around and not feel as if you have missed anything.

So, sit back and enjoy the game!

Early Years
1919 to 1922

1919:

The St. Mary's Lyceum baseball team was in the 18-20 year old age class of the Independent League in Pittsburgh, Pennsylvania. They were actually in McKees Rocks which is a suburb of Pittsburgh. St. Mary's was the local Catholic Church so they were coached by a priest, Father Baumer. This is where Joe, like his peers, first started to play organized baseball. He started out playing 1st base and a little bit in the outfielder. Later on he shifted into pitching and this is the position that he would eventually perfect.

Just as an interesting note, the word lyceum refers to an educational institution. It isn't used much now days but back in the early 1900's it was commonly used to designate a team affiliated with a school.

St. Mary's played teams in the Pittsburgh area and considered themselves as a first-rate squad. And in such stipulated in the newspaper that they only played teams of a high caliber. And that was how they kept their fans happy. They had a loyal fan base that would pay to watch them play at home on Bradley Field or travel to watch them play. And in order to have a good following they had to be good and play good teams.

Baseball was part business and part fun in these days. Teams were constantly forming and disbanding as sponsorships appeared and disappeared. And you needed a sponsor to be able to afford to field a team. Teams not only scheduled you to play based on your ability, but also because of the size of your following. The more fans you had the more the game made in gate revenue.

Pittsburgh was booming in 1919. Steel and coal were driving a surging economy, the Great War was ending, and the roaring 20's were getting started. People had jobs, money and were looking for entertainment in their off time. There wasn't TV yet and no one wanted to sit at home listening to the radio on a nice summer evening or weekend. People wanted to get out and have fun. And baseball was a great escape.

One of the best games Joe played in during this season was against the Coraopolis All-Stars. St. Mary's beat them 16-2 and Joe had 2 hits driving in 3 runs with a homerun. The box score said that *"In the sixth Semler drove the ball into the creek for a home run, making the longest hit of the season."*[3]

St. Mary's had played exceptional baseball over the summer having won 20 games and losing 4. And with that great season under their belt, they took that clout and secured a game with one of the best teams in the area, the Graybers. There was a lot of press coverage leading up to the game and probably the best was this one from the Pittsburgh Press;

"Westend baseball fans will assemble at Grayber Field in big numbers this afternoon to witness the game between the St. Mary's Lyceum Club and the Graybers. These clubs are the leading baseball representatives of that district this season. Their fields are just a short distance apart and there is much rivalry existing. St. Mary's has been trying for a long while to get a game with the Esplen club but was not successful until this week, and the boys from McKees Rocks district are going into the game this afternoon determined to put forth every effort to carry off a victory.

The lineup with such stars as the Laurent brothers and Marty Herbst back, is strong, and the bench of fast independent players that is to be found in Grayber uniforms is sure to be hard pressed for victory. Other St. Mary's players are Semler, Gauley, Boehm, Graff and Kleber. The Graybers will have their usual galaxy of stars on the diamond and an interesting contest is anticipated."[20]

The game was played on Sunday the 24th to a huge crowd. Like the article stated their fields were close to each other so their fan base was right at hand. But they did have people coming from all over the area and in one article they gave alternate travel routes by ferry and bus because there was a streetcar strike planned for that weekend.

St. Mary's started a pitcher from Lawrenceville by the name of Strobel and the Graybers started their ace southpaw "Lefty" Archer. These two guys had a pitching duel going on and the game was scoreless going into the top of the 8th inning when the Graybers came up to bat. Archer reached 1st base on an error by St. Mary's 2nd baseman Cauley, which was their only error of the game. Then the Graybers left fielder Bretch singled and Archer tried to make it all the way home on the hit. As he came sliding into home plate, he was tagged out in what was described as the prettiest play of the season!

The game stayed scoreless into the top of the 9th inning when the Graybers managed to get a run across in what would be the winning run. Archer ended up pitching a no-hit scoreless game and Strobel only allowed 4 hits. It was a loss for St. Mary's but they walked away with their heads high demonstrating that they could hang with the big boys. Joe played right field and went hitless.

The Graybers game didn't end the season for St. Mary's and they looked for another team to play that was just as popular. That team was the famous Negro League Homestead Grays. Baseball teams were segregated, but playing them was fair game. And the Homestead Grays were hugely popular in the Pittsburgh area. Because blacks couldn't play in the major leagues their teams had tremendous talent.

They originally meet at Bradley Field on Sunday August the 31st and with St. Mary's ahead in the 4th inning the game was called due to rain. The game was rescheduled for Sunday the 21st of September with "Lefty" Williams starting for the Grays and "Lefty" Archer starting for St. Mary's. Yes, that's the same pitcher that pitched for Grayber in that big game against St. Mary's. They had recruited him to play for them in this game. Bringing in a ringer like that wouldn't be allowed in normal league play, but this was unofficial exhibition ball!

Archer didn't start out as well as he did back in August and immediately gave up 3 runs in the top of the 1st inning. The game stayed at 3-0 until the top of the 7th inning when the Grays scored another run to make it 4-0. St. Mary's bats finally came alive in the bottom of the 7th inning for 1 run to make it 4-1. And that would be how it ended. Joe played right field again in this game and was hitless.

Here is a listing of some of St. Mary's games for 1919. There was no official listing and this is what I compiled from newspapers;

Spalding Athletics	0	St. Mary's	8	3 May
Larson Athletics	2	St. Mary's	12	17 May
Stromberg	2	St. May's	8	31 May
W. F. Drummers	12	St. Mary's	3	3 June
Lyceum All-Stars	4	St. Mary's	16	7 June

Braddock	6	St. Mary's	8	15 June
Coraopolis All-Stars	2	St. Mary's	16	19 June
Turtle Creek	5	St. Mary's	11	22 June
South Pittsburgh	2	St. Mary's	8	29 June
West Park	8	St. Mary's	17	5 July
McKay Chain Works	2	St. Mary's	5	13 July*[1]
McKay Chain Works	4	St. Mary's	3	16 July
Keck All-Stars	0	St. Mary's	3	19 July
Westinghouse	7	St. Mary's	8	26 July*[2]
Lemington Club	2	St. Mary's	5	2 Aug *[3]
Troy Hill	5	St. Mary's	18	9 Aug
American Railway	1	St. Mary's	10	16 Aug
Sheridan All Stars	5	St. Mary's	12	23 Aug
Graybers	1	St. Mary's	0	24 Aug
Homestead Grays	4	St. Mary's	1	21 Sept

*[1] Joe had 6 strikeouts

*[2] Joe had 6 strikeouts

*[3] Joe had 9 strikeouts

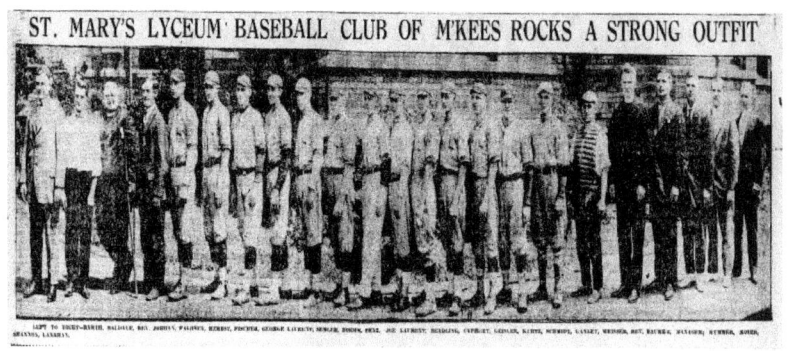

St. Mary's Lyceum 1919 team[19]

This picture was taken just after their big game with Grayber. Pictured left to right are: Barth, Baldauf, Rev. Jorden, Faloney, Herbst, Fisher, Geore Laurent, Semler, Boehm, Penz, Joe Laurent, Beadling, Cyphert, Geisler, Kurtz, Schmidt, Ganley, Weisser, Rev. Baumer (manager), Kummer, Moser.

1920:

Joe played for both St. Vincent's Lyceum and St. Mary's Lyceum again in the amateur Independent league. He started off with St. Vincent until St. Mary's started their season on the 16th of May but seemed to jump back and forth between teams during the season. Still playing a lot at first base he also started becoming more of a starting pitcher.

For some reason St. Mary's didn't pick up where they left off last season in respect to booking quality clubs to play. I think this had a lot to do with only Joe and two other players returning from last year's squad; one of the Laurent brothers playing 2nd base and Cyphert catching. The difficulty in obtaining games was to the point that St. Mary's was still running ads in the paper looking for a team to open up against all the way to the week prior to opening day. They eventually found a team but it was last minute and the club was an unknown team with little fan support.

They also didn't play near as well as last year and their schedule was light with a lot of missed games. They had several teams scheduled for July, such as Mt. Washington on the 11th and St. Luke's on the 18th, but they never played the games - probably due to weather. And that's about how the year went for St. Mary's - with a sporadic schedule and a lackluster season.

But playing adult baseball wasn't easy. Games were played in the evenings and on the weekends to work around the players work schedules. These men had jobs and baseball was more or less a pastime. Games generally started no later than 6pm on weekdays to enable getting a 9 inning game in. But getting off of work at 5pm or 5:30 and getting to the ball field by 6pm was a tight squeeze. So, a lot of games didn't start until after 6pm and only lasted 7 innings. The majority of games were held on the weekends, but with limited field space only so many teams could play.

The most interesting game for Joe this year was against the Salisbury A.A. when he pitched for St. Vincent's. It was a long 14 inning game which they eventually lost 4-3, but the stats were pretty amazing. Joe ended up with 10 strikeouts and the opposing pitcher, named Helsel, had 29 strikeouts!

Unfortunately, there was no big playoff game like last year. The season ended with St. Mary's playing St. Vincent in a Catholic duel at McKees Rocks. Playing at Bradley Park Joe pitched for St. Mary's and Mareski for St. Vincent's. The game was tight and was tied 4-4 after 4 innings. By the top of the 6th inning St. Vincent's was pulling away 8-4 but St. Mary's came back in the bottom of the same inning to close the gap and make it an 8-7 game. But that's all St. Mary's could muster and St. Vincent took the win. Joe had 6 strikeouts and Mareski 5 strikeouts.

Here is a listing of some of their games for 1920. Again, there is no official listing and this is what I compiled from newspapers;

Willcock	3	St. Vincent's	8	25 April*[1]
Salisbury A.A.	4	St. Vincent's	3	1 May
Korch Crescents	13	St. Vincent's	5	8 May*[2]
F.J. Broads	11	St. Vincent's	3	8 May
Dengler Club	0	St. Mary's	2	16 May*[3]
Lemington	3	St. Mary's	2	22 May
Carnegie Triangle	2	St. Mary's	18	28 May
Troy Hill	4	St. Vincent's	1	27 Aug
St. Vincents	8	St. Mary's	7	12 Sept

*[1] St. Vincent Lyceum season opener

*[2] Joe did not play

*[3] St. Mary's Lyceum season opener

1921:

Joe moved from the McKees Rocks Church League to the semi-pro South Hills League in 1921. He was now playing for the Mt. Washington K.O.K.A (Knights Of King Arthur) squad. They didn't have a home field because they were considered a traveling team, but they did play a majority of their games at Olympia Park which is located atop Mt. Washington and was locally referred to as Coal Hill.

The South Hills League in 1921 was made up of the following teams; Knoxville, McPirdles, Lineys, McKinleys, West End, Mt. Washington Lyceum, Brookline, and the Mt. Washington K.O.K.A. Knights. They played on Tuesday, Thursday, and Saturday. It's also interesting that the Knights manager, T. H Boehmer would place an ad in the Pittsburgh Press newspaper with the day's lineup and where to report. For example, on the 30th of June it read; *"K.O.K.A club will play Spang-Chalfant at Etna tonight at 6:30 pm sharp. The following players report at Jenkins Arcade at 5:15 pm: Strott, Semler, Keefe, Thomas, Laughlin, Beadling, Christy, Kelly, Hoffner, D. Ozborne and E. Ozbourne."*

You'll have to remember that a lot of people didn't have phones in 1922. So, an easy way to get in touch with people was to place an ad in the paper.

Olympia Park[4]

Joe opened the season with a bang on the 5th of May. Behind his pitching the Knights beat Spang-Chalfant 7-4 in a long 11 inning game. Spang jumped out first scoring 2 runs in the 3rd inning. But in the 5th inning the Knights scored 4 runs with the help of a homer from Joe with a man on base. Spang closed the gap in the 6th inning with a run and in the 8th inning with another one to tie the game. Finally in the 11th inning the Knights scored 3 runs to seal the win. Along with Joe's homer and run batted in he had 4 strikeouts.

Joe pitched a win with a 6-2 decision over fellow Mt. Washington team the Lyceum on Tuesday the 10th of May. Joe worked a fantastic 9 innings at Olympia Park allowing only 4 hits. He rounded out his fine pitching with 6 strikeouts. Here is the box score for this game to give you an example of what a typical box score in the paper would look like;

> The Mt. Washington K. O. K. A. club defeated Doc Jennings' Mt. Washington Lyceum. 6-2, in a hard fought battle at Olympia park last night. Semler had the Lyceum boys at his mercy throughout, striking out six and allowing but four hits. Thomas' home run with two men on and Keefe's hitting featured. K. O. K. A plays Brookline Thursday at West End. The score:

K. O. K. A.	R.	B.	P.	A.	E.	Lyceum	R.	B.	P.	A.	E.
Keefe.s	1	3	2	1	0	Wolfe.2.	0	0	4	1	0
Eisen.l.	2	1	0	0	0	Crove.l.	0	0	0	0	0
Beadl.3	1	2	2	2	0	Leac.3-s	1	1	3	2	0
Thoma.1	2	2	5	0	0	Car.m-1.	1	1	1	2	0
Strott.c	0	0	7	0	0	Erkle.s.	0	0	0	1	0
Laugh.2	0	2	1	1	0	B.O'Br.3	0	0	0	0	0
Christ.m	0	2	1	0	0	Ferric.1.	0	1	4	2	0
Osborn.r	0	0	0	0	0	Dailey.r	0	0	2	1	1
Semle.p	0	0	0	2	0	R.O'Br.c	0	0	4	1	1
						Reilly.p	0	0	0	0	0
						H.O'B.m	0	1	0	0	0
Total	6	12	18	6	0	Total	2	4	18	10	2

> K. O. K. A. ....3 0 0 0 1 2—6
> Lyceum ....0 0 0 2 0 0—2
> Two-base hit—Laughlin. Three-base hits—Keefe, Leach. Home run—Thomas. Stolen bases—Keefe, Laughlin, Christy. Double plays—Carey to Ferrick to Leach; Laughlin to Keefe. First base on balls—Off Semler 1, off Reilly 2, off Carey 2. Sacrifice—Laughlin. Struck out—By Semler 6, by Reilly 1, by Carey 3. Umpire—Ahearn.

Typical box score in the paper[6]

Another victory came in a hard fought game against Knoxville on the 28th of May. The game at McKinley Park was another great performance by Joe and put the Knights in 1st place in the

South Hills League. Knoxville scored a run in the 1st inning but the Knights came back in the 5th inning with two runs being driven in by Joe. In the 9th inning Joe hit a double and was later driven home for the final 2 runs. After the game the Knights announced they had signed a star Allegheny High School pitcher by the name of Steve Swetonic to their bull-pen of Joe, Carl Poke and Dutch Wilson. The 4 pitchers were said to be among the best in the area.

It was a bad day for the Knights when they dropped both games of a double header to Bellevue on the 31st of May. In the morning game Joe shared the pitching duties in a 14-9 loss. Offensively Joe had a hit, run batted in, and stole a base. In the evening game Joe also shared the pitching duties in the 8-0 shutout. Joe gave up 2 walks and got skunked at bat.

Playing on the 18th of June Joe led the Knights to a solid 6-2 victory over Troy Hill. Joe pitched a solid game with 12 strikeouts and only 1 walk. He helped his pitching game by hitting a double along with 2 hits and driving in a run.

Spang-Chalfant handed the Knights squad a loss on the 12th of July with a score of 6-3. Joe pitched the loss.

At this time in the season most leagues had player cutoff requirements in order to be eligible for the playoffs. Players had to be on a team's roster by the 1st of July and by mid-July teams had a 15 man roster limit. These rules helped prevent teams from stacking the deck towards the playoffs.

Playing away against Millvale on the 30th of July at Sample Hill Joe was in prime form throwing a 3 hitter. He rounded out the 12-3 performance with 12 strikeouts.

The Knights were handed another loss on the 20th of August by Fineview with a score of 6-2. Joe pitched the loss but squeaked out 2 strikeouts and spanked one for a double.

On the 23rd of August the knights hosted probably one of the best semi-pro clubs in western Pennsylvania, the Beaver Falls Elks. Just to give you an idea of the crowds they drew in, they were planning on 3,000 fans in the stands of Olympia Park and 5,000 overall.

The South Hills League championship was decided at Olympia Park on the 5th of September when the Knights and Lineys squared up for a doubleheader. It wasn't the Knights day and they dropped both games, 2-1 and 11-2. Joe helped pitch in the second game blowout. It wasn't his day either and he offered an error and 3 walks.

With the Knights season over Joe kept busy pitching. Playing for the Lockhart Giants Joe pitched a loss to the Pittsburgh Keystones on the 19th of September. The 8-1 loss did produce 5 strikeouts for Joe and he gave up 2 walks.

1922:

The Knights held a meeting in early March to discuss the upcoming season. The semi-pro players agreed to be represented on the diamond by a strictly first-class group of players. After tryouts in April the players were chosen and Joe made the cut as a pitcher. They planned to play local Pittsburgh teams and also teams from Ohio.

Managing the newly named West End K.O.K.A was still handled by J. H. Boehmer. But they would now be owned and coached by Honus Wagner, the famous former Pittsburgh Pirate shortstop, who would also play first base. The squad was known as a traveling team and didn't have a home field. It was said that Honus Wagner was a businessman who always organized his teams into what was known as a "traveling team." This type of team didn't have a home field to escape paying a home field fee. This was a set amount of money paid by home teams to visiting teams because the home team was getting ticket revenue from the game. The only drawback from this type of a set up was that other teams didn't like to book traveling teams because they couldn't draw any money off of them. But if you were good enough and had something to draw in crowds, like great players or ex-great players, teams would book you because you brought in ticket revenue. And Honus Wagner was a huge crowd draw in the Pittsburgh area. Add in that he had great local talent playing with him and you had the recipe for a profitable club.

It's pretty amazing that at 48 years old Honus Wagner would still be playing baseball. In the picture on the following page, he is with his West End team and in comparison Joe Semler is 21 and his teammates are about the same age. So Honus is over twice their age and competing well. Although it wasn't the major leagues it really wasn't much easier in the semi-pros. And when you look at his stats, he wasn't just phoning it in, he was playing hard and coaching at the same time. Honus was a big attraction during his days with the Pirates and he was still drawing in the crowds with West End. And the sports writers didn't miss an opportunity to mention him in the papers.

To make Honus Wagners team you had to be the best in the area. Honus had his baseball image to uphold. He was one of the first 5 players inducted in the baseball Hall of Fame in 1936 and had the second highest votes of those 5 inductees. And the man still makes the news today with the record breaking amount of money his baseball card keeps selling for. In 2016 it sold for over $3 million dollars.

Practice for the knights started in April but bad weather kept it limited. When they were able to get it in they meet on Tuesday's, Thursday's and Saturday's at the Denny Grounds.

In the season opener against Bellevue on April the 29th Joe shared 1st base duties with Honus Wagner. The 48 year old had a great day against Bellevue. With 4 at bats, he had a double and drove in a run and Joe helped out with a hit. In the end it wasn't enough and the West End team lost 13-1.

West End Team 1922[5]

Back row left to right: Barum, Rosenberger, Laughlin, J.M. Boehmer (in suit), Strott, Semler, and Hewlett. Middle row left to right: Douglas, Reidel, Honus Wagner, Blazing, and H. Allen. Front row left to right: Beadling and Friesel.

Getting back to pitching Joe took the mound against the Mt. Washington Scholastics on the 7th of May. Playing back at Olympia Park Joe fanned 18 with only 2 walks. Offensively he was on fire stroking out a triple and a double on 4 at bats.

Once again Joe struck out 18 on the 28th of May against the Bank of Pittsburgh team. Joe threw a shutout winning 9-0. He also helped himself out with a hit that drove in 2 runs.

Meeting the Pleasant Valley Smilers on the 31st of May the West End team swept two games in a double header. Joe pitched the morning game squeaking out a 5-4 win. In the afternoon game he played middle field (now referred to as centerfield) and had a triple, double, and drove in a run to help the team with a 10-2 win. Honus Wagner was once again playing 1st base.

In June Joe started sharing his playing duties with the Beaver Falls Elks. It would be the start of a long relationship with a great club. But on the 25th he had a rough start. Playing the W.M. Turners of Wilkinsburg the starting pitcher was rocked for 5 runs in the 1st inning. Ed Harvey, the manager of the Elks, pulled the starter and sent in Joe. He gave up 3 more runs to the Turners and the Elks lost 8-1.

Back playing for the West End on the 27th they were matched up against the Mt. Washington Kaceys in a highly touted match. The game was played at Olympia Park and drew a huge crowd. Honus Wagner was playing 1st base and Joe was pitching. Joe got rocked pretty hard in the first 2 innings for 5 runs. He settled down and only gave up another run over the next 7 innings. But it was too much for West End to come back from and they lost 6-2. Joe did have 6 strikeouts and a hit in the game.

Beaver Falls Elks & Bellevue 1922-1928

The Beaver Falls Elks were a premier semi-pro team in the 1920's and were very popular in the area. Just 40 miles outside of Pittsburgh they had a big fan base. A lot of this had to do with their fine baseball playing but also because they played the best teams in the area to include the Homestead Grays in the Negro League.

Joe was one of their star pitchers at the time. Their one time manager Ed Harvey said that *"Joe Semler and Ed (Count) Hilty were the two best pitchers he ever managed."*[1] And what made Joe a good pitcher? Well, he was known for good control of the ball, a nice fastball, and most of all his curve ball.

I remember in High School trying out for our Junior Varsity Baseball team. I had asked Joe to show me how to throw a curve ball, which he did, along with a knuckle ball which are some nifty pitches. These types of pitches are difficult and take a lot of practice to master. Joe had obviously honed his skill back with St. Mary's and the K.O.K.A squads with these. Now he was playing with some of the best players in semi-pro ball and you had to be good or you wouldn't last long.

And that was how you moved up the baseball ladder. You started with a local team playing semi-pro A, AA, and Triple-A ball and then hopefully made the jump into the minor leagues and then the majors. Sure, some guys jumped levels but you had to be extremely talented to do that. So, Joe made the jump into Triple-A ball with the Elks.

And in doing so he signed a contract locking him into playing that season with them. He still had his primary job as a carpenter but this was extra money to be made during the baseball season which ran from April through September. Games with the Elks were held in the evenings around 6:30 and on Saturday's. Not only did this accommodate the players, but it's when people were typically off of work and could fill the stands.

1922:

On June the 22nd the Elks lost against the W.M Turners of Wilkinsburg 8-1. Joe came in relief after the starter was banged up for 5 runs in the 1st inning. Joe gave up 2 walks and had a hit.

Playing at home on the 29th of July the Elks met up with the Glassport Patricians in a tight match which was pretty much sealed up in the 1st inning when the Elks Mickey McBride hit a 3 run homer to lead the team to a 3-1 victory. Joe pitched the game getting 3 strikeouts.

The Elks handed the Damascus Steelers a 7-0 shutout on the 9th of August. Joe only gave up 3 hits in the game and offensively had 2 hits, one for a double, and drove in a run.

This picture was taken in 1922 when Joe was still playing for both West End and the Elks

Left to right: Semler, McGinley, Walsh, Polk, and McBride

Playing 1st base Joe hit a home run and drove in a run in the Elks 4-2 victory over the McKinley Club. Playing at

McKinley Park in front of one of the largest crowds in years Joe also helped out in a double play.

In a double header against the Warren Moose team on the 4th of September the Elks swept both games. Joe sat out the morning game which they won 10-3 and pitched a 5 hitter in the afternoon which helped the Elks seal a tight 2-1 win. Joe stuck out 8.

Just two days later on the 6th of September Joe split the pitching duties in a win over the Jeannette A.A. The Elks rolled up the 6-3 victory with the help of a hit and run driven in by Joe.

Just three days later the Elks played the first of three games of the National Baseball Federations Semi-Pro Inter City Series. The Elks who were the semi-professional champions of the Greater Pittsburgh Baseball Commission were going up against the Cleveland Tillings who were that areas Class-AA and Triple-A champions. They also fielded some former major league players to include Terry Turner at 3rd base who was a former Pittsburgh Pirate.

Playing the first game in Beaver Falls Carl Poke started on the mound for the Elks but only lasted into the 2nd inning. After giving up 3 runs he was replaced by Joe, who was undoubtedly in his biggest game to date. Joe pitched a great game into the 7th inning and things remained close. In the bottom of the 7th Joe helped his cause with a double followed by a single from Bronson Reese. Tommy Young brought them all home with a homer and the Elks took the lead. But Cleveland came back and sealed the win in the 8th inning with a 9-6 victory.

The next morning the Elks boarded a P. &L.E. train to play the remaining 2 games in a double header at Dunn Field in Cleveland to decide the series. The Elks went on to sweep Tillings 7-4 and 10-6 with both games being pitched by Johnny Pearson. What an arm that guy must have had to pitch back to back morning and afternoon games against a premier team.

The series victory propelled the Elks, who were the defending champions, onto the finals in the Inter City Series. Drawing a bye, they continued playing regular games in their local league as well. And Joe got the call on the 16th in Beaver Falls against the Even City Athletics. After 5 tough innings he was pulled and Carl Poke came into relieve him. But the damage was already done and the Elks lost 5-2.

That week the Elks found out they would be playing the Price Hills squad of Cincinnati in the Triple-A Championship Series of the National Baseball Federation. The first game would be at home in Beaver Falls and it was expected to draw the biggest crowd ever.

Although Joe was mentioned several times in articles leading up to the series as being in Ed Harvey's stable of pitchers he unfortunately didn't play in the series. Probably because the veteran players were started.

The series was swept by the Elks in a 4-2 win on the 23rd of September and 7-1 and 10-2 wins in a double header in

Cincinnati on the 24th. There was some drama in the series when Price Hills challenged the Elks winning the first game in Cincinnati. They filed a protest that the Elks pitcher wasn't eligible to play in the series because he hadn't played enough qualifying regular season games. The protest was overturned and the Elks were crowned champions.

1922 Beaver Falls Elks Championship Team[48]

Pictured above are back row left to right: Carl Poke, Carl Anderson, Joe Semler, Harry "Mickey" McBride, Harry E. McGinley, Lee Macley, and Earl V. Croud. Front row left to right: Bronson Reese, Edward Kelly, J.H. Beeson, Thomas R. Young, Fred Ward, and Richard A. "Ziggie" Walsh.

The following day they returned home to a huge celebration. It started off with a parade in which the Elks were driven through town while a 40 piece brass band played. That evening a banquet was held in their honor at the Elks clubhouse. Music was provided by Danny Nirella and his jazz orchestra. Among the guest speakers was the great baseball player Ty Cobb, who was currently coaching the Detroit Tigers. The evening ended with the players being presented gift baskets adorned with the Elks colors and a silver dollar.

1923:

The Elks opened the season on April the 28th at home against the J.J. Deans. A light rain didn't prevent the teams from playing and the Triple-A champion Elks were eager to get going again. Under the management of Jimmy Beeson the Elks fell behind the Deans and things looked bad. In the top of the 5th inning they were behind by a run and there were 2 Deans on base. Beeson decided to pull his starter and Joe came in relief. He made quick work out of the Deans and got the Elks out of the inning without any harm. The Elks took advantage of the situation in the bottom of the 5th inning when Ed Kelly doubled and Tommy Young scored him on a single. Young then stole second and Red Kirk drove them home with a homer to seal the game at 4-2. Joe held the Deans at bay with 8 strikeouts in just 4-1/3 innings.

Getting the start at home on the 5th of May against the Broadway Club of Beachwood Joe didn't disappoint the home crowd. He held the visitors to 2 hits and fanned 16 batters in an 11-0 win.

At home against the Christy Park club of McKeesport on the 19th of May the Elks almost let one slip by them. Starting pitcher Irwin took the Elks through the 6th inning giving up 3 runs and 3 hits. Jannuzzi was brought in as relief and lost control of the game letting Christy Park score 4 runs in the next inning. He was pulled and Joe came in relief. He calmed things down with 3 strikeouts to give the Elks an 11-8 win.

Playing Union Tool from Carnegie at home on the 2nd of June Joe got the start. He pitched into the 7th inning but Union Tool was ahead 3-2 and manager Beeson pulled him for Joe Drugmond. He held Union Tool in check while the Elks came back to claim their 5th straight win with a score of 4-3.

Joe went all 9 innings against the McKinley squad on the 10th of June. Striking out 5 he held McKinley to only 2 runs in the Elks 7-2 victory.

Getting the call again on the 23rd Joe let the Braddock Elks only get 6 hits off of him as he went all 9 innings for the Beaver Falls Elks. Throwing 6 strikeouts to add to his performance he led his team to a 7-2 victory.

1923 Beaver Falls Elks[7]

Top left to right: Joe Semler, Ziggy Walsh, Chick Croud, Tommy Young, and Dewey McGinley. Bottom left to right: Jay Red Kirk, Jim Henderson, Joe Lefty Drugmond, Eddie Kelly, and Jim Beeson.

This article from Fred P Alger in the Pittsburgh Daily Post on the 24th of June 1923 accompanied the photo above and summarizes the club perfectly.

"Out for another world's championship. Thus Jimmy Beeson and his Beaver Falls Elks team express themselves while playing the same kind of ball that brought them two championships in the National Baseball Federation and which has kept them at the top of the heap in Western Pennsylvania circles for some time. Just as most title-contending ball clubs, the Beaver Falls team is not a club that wins every game it plays, but the season's average of victories keeps them well at the top, and there are few teams that can claim any number of victories over this crack aggregation of ball tossers.

In Joe Drugmond the Elks have one of the best lefthanders of this section and a lad who pitched the Beaver Falls team to their championship back in 1921 and then took a year's grace in the Western and other circuits. Joe is back with the Elks this season and going better than ever, which means that he is at his best form.

Paul McCollough, a New Castle lad, who has been pastiming in the American Association for the past few years is another ace flinger. Another young pitcher showing much promise of developing into a star is Joe Semler, the McKees Rocks lad, who has been on the Elks' roster for the past two seasons.

Behind the bat the champions have two great receivers in Ziggy Walsh and Jimmy Henderson, both of Homestead, and two better catchers would be hard to find. At first Chick Croud holds down the bag in approved fashion, while the remainder of the infield would be hard to equal in local ranks. Joe White, Jimmy Beeson, Tommy Young and Dewey McGinley form a combination that few clubs can boast of. Eddie Kelly, G. McCullough and several other outfielders round the combination that the Elks have representing them this season.

Nothing short of another championship will satisfy the team which went through the best in the country in the past two years and brought to this section the first title of National champions."

The Elks hosted the major league Cincinnati Reds on the 27th of June. Joe got the start against the big leaguers and held them scoreless with only 2 hits going into the 7th inning. But the pros finally got to Joe and roughed him up for 4 runs, closing the Elks lead to 2. Joe Drugmond came in relief and allowed only 1 more run in the Elks 8-5 win.

That had to be the highlight of Joe Semler's pitching career up until this point. I can't find that he pitched against any other major league team yet and he did a fantastic job pitching a 2 hit shutout going into the 7th inning. The Reds at the time had finished in 2nd place the previous year in the National League and would go on to take 2nd place again this year. Finishing up 1923 with a record of 91-63 they were no slack team to pitch against.

With three days of rest Joe was back on the mound against the National Tube team out of McKeesport. It was hailed as the fastest game of the season as Joe only faced 28 batters. Holding the visitors to only two scattered singles and racking up 1 strikeout Joe went the distance in the 2-0 win.

Again, on the 4th of July the Elks continued their winning streak at home by defeating the Teser Club of Homewood in a double header by the scores of 3-2 and 5-3. Joe got the nod in the morning game and was matched up against Carl Stewart, who was noted for his spitball and claimed to be the ace of pitchers in the independent league. Joe wasn't rattled and let his strong right arm hold the Tesers to only 5 hits and racked up 4 strikeouts in the 3-2 win.

Up against the J.J. Dean's again on the 12th of July Joe was the center of attention in front of a crowd of 6,000. And they were thrilled to see their rising star pitcher throw a 12-0 shutout along with 8 strikeouts.

The Rochester Terminals shocked a hometown crowd of 2,000 on the 18th of July when they handed the Elks their first defeat at home in 18 games there. Joe was one of three pitchers that couldn't slow down the Terminals in their 7-3 win.

On the 21st of July the Elks played the Negro League Homestead Grays. The game was held at the Pittsburgh Pirates ball field, Forbes Field, and was attended by a crowd of around 5,000 who wanted to see the area's finest black and white players. Johnny Pearson, who threw those two great games in the lead up to last year's Triple-A championship game against Tillings was expected to get the start. He was just getting back from trying out with the Pirates and was relegated to right field and Paul McCollough was given the starting pitching job. The game was close going into the 6th inning with the Elks leading 4-3. But the Grays bats got hot and the Elks made some critical fielding errors giving up 4 runs in the inning. Joe was brought in relief but his strong right arm wasn't enough. He ended up conceding another run and the Gays won 8-4. Walter Cannady closed it for the Grays and held the Elks scoreless to the end.

This type of game between white and black players wasn't that unusual in the Pittsburgh area during the days of segregation. It was obviously a big fan draw and would easily fill up major league stadiums like Forbes Field. It was the only chance you were going to get to see elite black and white ball players go at it on the ball field.

1923 Homestead Grays

The partial picture of the Homestead Grays on the previous page shows some of the Grays that played the Elks on the 21st at Forbes Field. They are left to right: Dave Brown played shortstop, W. Harris pinch hit, Bill Johnson played catcher, Forrest Mashaw did not play, Willis Moody played 1st base, Moe Harris 2nd base, Cum Posey did not play, and Walter Cannady closed the game out as pitcher.

The 31st of July was tough on the Elks and they lost a tight one against one of the better teams in the area, Bellevue. Playing on the road the Elks were greeted by the biggest crowd Bellevue had amassed all year and they wanted to get a look at the Triple-A champs. It was a tight one and Joe had only given up one run after 7 inning and the game was tied. But he gave up another run in the 8th inning and one in the 9th inning to lose 3-2. Bellevue was on a roll and the win made it 25 in a row for them.

It was a battle of the Elks as Beaver Falls traveled to Edgar Thomson Park to play the Braddock Elks. And it was a left handed dual between Beavers Joe Drugmond and Braddock's Abe Martin. The game played on the 16th of August set Beaver Falls back another game as they lost a nail biter 1-0. Drugmond managed 8 strikeouts and Joe Semler had 2 in relief.

It wasn't getting any easier as the Elks headed into the home stretch of the season on the 25th of August and once again met the Homestead Grays at Forbes Field. In front of a crowd of well over 4,000 Joe got the start and was bruised up pretty good giving up 2 runs in the 4th inning. The Elks were getting skunked and remained hitless after 5 innings against the Grays speed baller Oscar Owens. When Joe gave up another run in the 5th inning he was relieved by lefty Drugmond. But even he couldn't hold off the Grays bats and they scored 3 more runs before the 6-2 final. Brown, Harris, Johnson, Moody, Moe Harris, and Cannady all played in this game as well. After beating the Elks the Grays, with Owens pitching again, went on to beat the club from Fineview 11- 4 in the second half of a double header.

The Elks were set to defend their National Baseball Federation title on the 11th of September when they played the Harmarville Consumers. In front of a rowdy crowd of over 10,000 fans the event took place at Edgar Thomas Park on a chilly and damp night. The large crowd brought in $865.85 of gate revenue. Johnny Pearson was started for the Elks and the underdog Consumers were leading 3-2 by the end of the 6th inning. Pearson couldn't keep them in check and the Consumers scored 3 more runs to win 6-4 and advance in the playoffs. It was a huge let down for the favored Elks who had won the championship the past two years. The Consumers went on to play the Baltimore Alcos. Joe Semler didn't participate in the loss which was full of accusations by the Consumers that Pearson was doctoring the ball and by the Elks that the Consumers were playing ineligible players. The Consumers went on to lose in the Inter-City round.

The picture on the next page was in the newspaper the day of the game and shows the Elks, top row left to right: White,

Semler, Drugmond, McGinley, Croud, Kelly, Paul McCoullough, White, Kirk, Young, Beeson, and Stan McCollough. The Consumers middle row left to right: Murray, Bright, Wentzel, Joe Doherty, Bill Edwards, Ray Schultise, Ray Page, and Bill White. Bottom row Left to right: Jimmy Beeson the manager of the Elks, Jo Doherty manager of Consumers, Lefty Drugmond of the Elks, Paul McCoullough of the Elks and Johnny Pearson of the Elks.

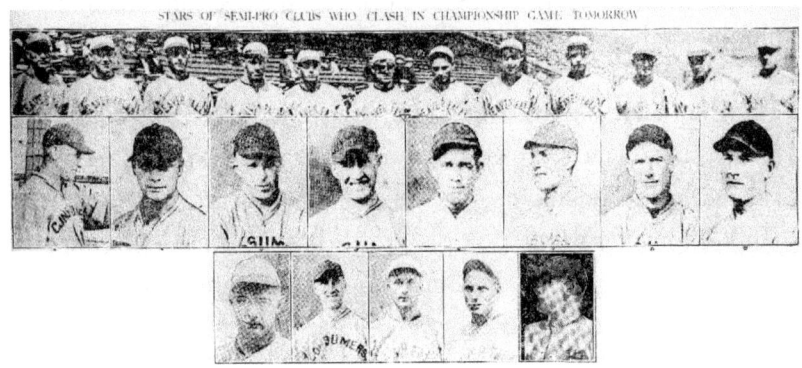

Elks and Consumers Teams 1923[9]

The Independent League had a few more games before the end of the season and Joe pitched his last game of the season on the 23rd of September. It ended on a bad note with the Elks losing to the Sharon Elks 9-3. Johnny Pearson started but was relieved by Joe who had 5 strikeouts.

1924:

After a disappointing season the Elks shook things up and announced in February that they were replacing their coach

Jimmie Beeson with Leo Mackey who had brought them their first semi-pro championship in 1921. He wouldn't be the only new face. He was bringing a young kid named Haines with him who was a promising pitcher from Lancaster, Ohio. And Gene Gahles a catcher from the University of Pittsburgh who had turned down some minor league offers to stay and play for the Elks. He had also played for the Elks during their 1921 champion season. Tommy Young, Chick Cloud, Stan McCullough and Dewey McGinley would also return from last season. Joe Semler and Eddie Kelly were rumored to be signing with a team from Decatur, Illinois. Johnny Pearson had signed with the Rochester Reds, Ziggy Walsh with the rival Braddock Elks and Joe "Lefty" Drugmond was up in the air.

The team had also locked in an agreement to play games against the Rochester Reds, Braddock Elks, Bellevue and the North Side Board of Trade. This is how teams ensured they played other high quality teams that would draw crowds and revenue. They tried to book the best they could in and outside of their League.

In April the Elks sealed the deal on their pitching roster by signing Joe Semler and Jimmy Uchrinsko. Joe had many offers from other Independents and minor league clubs but turned them down to play for the Elks again. It was big news in the area and his signing made the major newspapers in Pittsburgh. It was said that Joe *"has about as pretty a curve ball as any pitcher in this section can boast of and he possesses the head to mix them up enough to fool opposing batsmen."*[8]

You may be asking yourself why Joe would turn down a minor league deal if that's the next step up and obviously where everyone wants to move up to. Well Joe had just gotten married and had his first child due in July. So, I think he wanted to stay close to home.

The Elks held their last team practice on the 26th of April and played their first game at home on Saturday the 3rd of May against the C.M.C club of Homestead. Jimmy Uchrinsko started the season opener with a 7-1 win.

The Elks traveled to Warren, Ohio the following day to play the Warren Moose squad. Joe got the start and went all 9 inning holding the strong Moose club to just 2 runs in a 3-2 win.

Joe worked his first home game of the season on the 17th of May and held the Finkelhors to only 1 hit in 5 innings and sent 5 of the visitors to the dugout on strikeouts. After piling up an 8 run lead in the 5th inning Joe was relieved by Williams who kept the 16-3 win.

With Joe pitching superb ball on the 22nd of May the Elks pulled off a nice victory over the Homewood Tesers at Homewood. In front of a large Homewood crowd Joe held the Tesers scoreless for the first 6 innings. But in the 7th inning they roughed him up for 3 runs. It wasn't enough though and the Elks pulled off the 5-3 win.

Getting the starting duties on the 31st of May Joe started against the Sharon Elks. Pitching the first game of a double header Joe held Sharon to one hit in a wonderfully pitched game that brought the Elks a 6-1 win. In the second game Jimmy Uchrinsko pitched a 6-5 win for the sweep.

It was a nail biter at the North Borough for a Thursday evening game against Bellevue on the 5th of June. Joe got the start in what was to be one of the most thrilling nights in baseball for Bellevue in a while. Joe had gotten the Elks to the 9th inning with the game tied 6-6. The visiting Elks led off the 9th and scored a game leading run making it 7-6. Jimmy Uchrinsko was brought in to seal the game in the bottom of the 9th. But he let one slip for a 2 run homer that gave the Elks an upsetting last minute 8-7 loss.

It was the second time the Elks had meet their arch rivals the Harmarville Consumers who had snatched their chance to claim a third World Championship last year. The first meeting was back on the 7th of June when Jimmy Uchrinsko got the start in an away game in Harmarville. The consumers cleaned his clock in a 6-0 shutout. Just 10 days later on the 17th Joe would get the start and his chance to get revenge. But in front of the visitors' home fans he was sent to the showers after giving up 7 runs in the 7th inning. Jimmy Uchrinsko came in to close but the damage was done and the Elks dropped their second game of the season to the Consumers 8-4.

The picture on the following page are as follows. Back row left to right: Hud Ellis (Business manager), Young (manager) Semler, McCullough, Croud, McGinley, McBride, and Urinsko. Front row left to right: Musser, Wyssier, Snellbacher,

Sanders, Gaco (mascot), and Lane. I think it's interesting that the teams of this period had mascots, which would later be referred to as a ball or bat boy.

Beaver Falls Elks June 1924[10]

The following day it was also the second time the Elks had played the Warren, Ohio Moose this year. Joe Had beat them in his first game of the season. It was a hard fought battle in this one and it went back and forth in front of the Moose fans. Joe came in relief of Lane and the Elks bats came alive scoring in the 8th and 9th inning and the game came down to a 4-4 tie.

On a Sunday the 22nd of June Joe went the distance on the road in a 3-2 close win against Kinloch. With 5 strikeouts he held the home team scoreless until the 9th inning when he gave up the 2 runs.

The Sharon Elks were still upset from losing that double header back in May and were looking for revenge when they came into Beaver Falls on the 28th of June. Joe got the start and went all 9 innings with 4 strikeouts. But his teammates didn't help with 7 infield errors. In return Sharon handed Beaver Falls one of the worst beatings they had received at home in years, 11-4.

Joe went the distance against the Jeanette Independent team on July 2nd. In a powerful 6-1 win Joe threw a 2 hitter with 7 strikeouts.

With two days' rest Joe was on the mound again. The Elks were hosting the White Autos of Cleveland, Ohio in a double header. Jimmy Uchrinsko took the morning game easily winning it with a 3-1 win and giving up just 4 hits. Joe took the afternoon game and throwing 5 strikeouts beat Cleveland 6-5 in 11 innings.

On the road Joe took on the Clearys of Koppel, PA on the 10th of July. It was a tight game tied up at 3-3 going into the 9th inning. The Elks drove in 2 runs in the top of the 9th and Joe held the opponents scoreless in the bottom of the 9th for the win. Joe also had 7 strikeouts in the game.

Playing at Ambridge Joe Drugmond started and gave up a run in the 6th inning. The Elks battled it out to the last minute as they scored a run in the bottom of the 9th inning to tie the game 1-1. Joe Semler came in relief and held Ambridge scoreless to the end for the tie.

Joe had a short game on the 31st throwing 4 strikeouts and giving up just 2 hits in a 6 inning 2-1 win against Charleroi. When the game was called in the 6th inning due to rain the Elks had runners on 1st and 3rd with 2 outs. Games did get called due to rain or bad weather and also due to darkness. The first night games wouldn't be played until 1935 in the major leagues. Stadiums were also open to the elements and rain was a common cause of game delays and cancellations.

It was a nasty affair when the Elks traveled to Koppel to play the Clearys on August the 14th. Jim Uchrinsko immediately got clobbered giving up 2 runs in the 1st inning and 7 in the 2nd inning. Joe was brought in relief and he couldn't cool the red hot Koppel bats. Although the runs were not totally their fault because they weren't getting much help from their defense who committed 8 errors in the game. The game only went 7 innings but that was enough to leave the Elks with a 17-2 beating.

The Sharon Elks looking for another big win against the Elks came rolling into Beaver Falls on August the 23rd. Joe got the start and went all 9 innings in a pretty well pitched game. But he didn't get much offensive help and the Sharon squad had brought in a pitcher who was just released from last year's district champion Hamarville Consumers. Sharon got the 4-2 win and Joe walked away with a loss.

In the year's biggest game for the Elks on the 31th of August they hosted the Harmarville Consumers. It was the National Championship 3rd round elimination game. And since being eliminated by the Consumers last year the Elks wanted revenge. They had a better record going into the game at 31-12 with 4 ties verse the Consumers record of 33-28 with 7 ties. Jimmy Uchrinsko started and after getting roughed up was relieved by Joe "lefty" Drugmond. They couldn't stop the Consumers and they once again handed the Elks a 5-3 loss.

With inter-league play still going on the Elks hosted the Cleveland White Autos in a double header the following day. There was no rest for Jimmy Uchrinsko who got the start in the morning game and went all 9 innings in a 3-2 win. Joe took the afternoon game and went 9 innings striking out 7 in his 8-2 win for the sweep.

It was another double header against the Sharon Elks in Sharon on the 7th. Once again Jimmy Uchrinsko took the morning game duties and pitched all 9 innings for a 10-6 win. Joe took the agreed 7 inning afternoon game and struck out 5 for a 2-1 win and sweep.

As the 1924 season was winding down there was still the Beaver County Baseball title on the line. Ed Harvey, the off and on manager of the Elks, had compiled a team of some of the best players in the area to play against the Elks in a three game series for the County title. His team was known simply as the "Ed Harvey's." The Elks had won the first game played on September 6th and Joe "Lefty" Drugmond pitched the 3-2 win. The second game was held on the 13th of September and Joe Semler was given the start. Joe pitched a great game giving up just 3 hits in a 6-0 shutout. His win gave the Elks the Beaver County Title.

With the season at an end for the Independent League the pitching results were published in the Pittsburgh Daily Post.[11] And although being eliminated in the first round of championship play the Elks pitchers did pretty well. Joe "Lefty" Drugmond came in 7th with a record of 18-5 with 7 ties, Joe Semler came in 9th with a record of 13-4, Jimmy Uchrinsko came in 14th with a record of 18-8, and Walter Cannady of the Homestead Grays came in first with a record of 10-1.

1925

As the season was starting to unfold in February there were a lot of uncertainties with the future of the Beaver Falls Elks. The team hadn't formally organized for the upcoming season and there was even talk of them moving to a league in Eastern Ohio. None of the management had been established and stars like Joe Semler and Jimmy Uchrinsko were being courted to sign by other teams. In fact, the club from Bellevue was heavily soliciting Joe to sign.

And this wasn't unusual for teams of this period. Just like the Beaver Falls Elks who were sponsored by the Elks organization of Beaver Falls, every year teams had to lock in sponsors who were going to pay their salaries, hire managers, and coordinate teams to play.

Joe eventually signed with the Elks league rival the Bellevue club of the North Boroughs who would be playing in the Independent league. Joe would be teamed up with his old pitching buddy Carl Poke from his K.O.K.A and early Elks days. Managing Joe's new team would be Jim Greenbough and Jack Miller would be coaching. They were promising a good year and had at least 14 games a month scheduled during the season. They had already booked Joe's former Elks for 8 games, 6 with the Homestead Grays, 5 with Honus Wagner's team, 6 with Homestead, and 5 with National Tube.

In his debut for Bellevue Joe got the start against National Tube, who were celebrating their opening day at home in McKeesport on the 9th of May. Johnny Pearson was on the mound for the home team and gave up two homers. Joe was pitching a good game and was ahead 4-1 going into the 9th inning, but that's when it all started to unravel. After giving up 3 singles and hitting a batter Joe gave up 4 runs and chalked up a 5-4 loss.

Joe got his next start at home against the North Side Traders on the 16th. Starting off a bit shaky he gave up 3 runs in the 1st inning. But he settled down and only allowed the visitors to 5 hits in the game. The Bellevue bats answered with a run in the 1st inning and 3 more in the 3rd inning to secure a 4-3 win for Joe.

In front of a huge crowd at Forbes Field Joe got the start against the Homestead Grays on the 23rd of May. He went all 9 innings but the red hot Grays, who had already reached 23 wins so far this season, started out with 3 runs in the 1st inning. Joe stayed with it but just couldn't slow the Grays down and they went on to beat Joe 9-5.

Bellevue Club May 1925[12]

Pictured above are back row left to right: Carl Poke, Jack Miller, Hollis Cannon, Lee Cook, Cy Rheams, and John Lauer. Left to right front row: Joe Semler, Gene Steinbrenner, George Lees, Roy McKissock, and Bob Way.

Playing Woodlawn on the road Joe got the start and threw 5 strikeouts in a close game on June the 3rd. But it wasn't good enough and after going all 9 innings Joe put up a 5-3 loss.

Finally on the 13th Joe gets a decisive win with Bellevue in a brilliantly pitched 12-2 win on the road at Charleroi. Throwing a 2 hit game and sending 9 to the dugout on strikeouts he looked impressive. He even hit a home run!

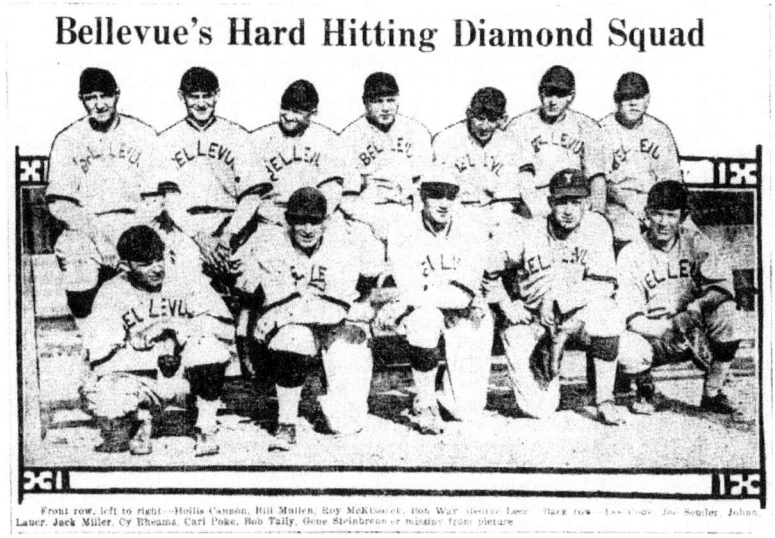

Bellevue Club June 1925[13]

Pictured above are front row left to right: Hollis Cannon, Bill Mullen, Roy McKissock, Bob Way, and George Lees. Back row left to right: Lee Cook, Joe Semler, Johnny Lauer, Jack Miller, Cy Rheams, Carl Poke, and Bob Tally.

Not wanting to leave the impression that game against Charleroi was a fluke Joe pitched another excellent game at home on the 18th. Playing against Munhall he kept them to only 7 hits and handed out 8 strikeouts in the 10-3 win.

Picking up where he left off Joe went against Martin Furniture on the 23rd at home. And the hometown fans loved watching Joe pitch an 8-1 win. Joe made it look easy by only allowing the visitors 6 hits and striking out 7.

A 4 run rally in the 9th inning helped Joe beat his old team mates the Beaver Falls Elks on the 30th of June. In a thrilling Tuesday night game at Bellevue Field Joe was pitching against his old team mate Joe "Lefty" Drugmond. Down 7-4 and going into the bottom of the 9th inning Elmer Wyssier led off the inning pinch hitting for Joe Semler. He put it over the fence to make it 7-5. Jim Beeson then walked followed by Cy Rheams. Jack Miller advanced both with a single to load the bases. Beeson scored with a hit by Hollis Cannon who was thrown out at 1st base making it 7-6. Bobby Way lifted one down the third base line for his third hit of the night driving in Rheam and Miller for the 8-7 win!

It must have been great for Joe to catch up with his old teammates. And I'm sure beating them was even all the better. And the teams that played in the Independent league were constantly shuffling players as the teams reorganized every year and players signed where they could get the best deal. So, they all knew each other pretty well as teammates, ex-teammates, and competitors that they played constantly.

And right after this game there was an article in the paper[14] about how the Elks wanted to make a trade to get Joe back. They were even willing to trade their star 3rd baseman Dewey McGinley to get him. Turns out Bellevue had just released their 3rd baseman Gene Steinbrenner and needed one. And the Elks were hurting for a premier pitcher. They had just lost their ace Charley Rohleder who they had acquired from the Appalachian League at the beginning of the year. He had just left in disgust after not being played enough and sitting 10 days on the bench without pitching a game. But strangely Bellevue ended up just releasing Joe and Carl Poke instead of trading them because they felt they were not pitching well.

Joe and Carl's last game with Bellevue was in a July 4th double header against the North Side Board of Trade. Bellevue came into the series winning 10 out of their last 11 games. Joe went all 9 innings in the morning game to win 11-6 and Carl Poke and George Lee split the pitching duties in the afternoon 8-7 win for the sweep. I wonder if Bellevue was rethinking their decision to release them.

At this point in the season several teams such as Ambridge and Charleroi were forced to drop out of the league and folded. It all boiled down to money and they said that they couldn't afford the $75 visiting team fee. This was a fee they had to pay visiting teams when they played a game at home. They said due to poor fan patronage they were not making enough to cover the fee and losing money on home games. Add in that they were also expected to pay their players on a Triple-A rating scale and it all added up to them going broke.

Joe moved back to the Beaver Falls Elks and you can see him in the following picture when the Elks met the North Side Board of Trade for a game on the 14th. Joe didn't get the start but he is back with the Elks.

Elks and Board of Trade before their 14 July game[15]

Playing at home on the 18th Joe got his first start back with the Elks and he proved himself by shutting out the Akron General Tire club 5-0. Joe went all 9 innings pitching a superb game and the papers said he looked like a major leaguer allowing only 2 hits and throwing 5 strikeouts.

It was a pitching duel on the 25th of July when National Tube of McKeesport came to Beaver Falls and faced Joe. He hadn't faced National Tube and Johnny Pearson since his debut with Bellevue back in May. He lost that game in the 9th inning. This game started out with a spectacular play by National Tubes Ernie Pratt who robbed Earl Cloud of a sure homer when he made a fantastic running catch. Although plays like that helped Pearson keep the Elks to only 3 hits, Joe only gave up 6 hits and the Elks prevailed in a 2-1 win.

Ending the month, the Elks went into Bellevue on the 31st. Joe got the start against his old teammates and it looked like it was going to be an early night as the Elks jumped out to an 8-0 lead in the 4th inning of a 6 inning game. But Joe fell apart giving up 7 runs in the bottom of the 4th inning making it an 8-7 game. Lefty Drugmond was brought in to close and even he couldn't pull off the win as the Elks fell 9-8.

Getting the start again at home the following day against Bellevue, Joe wanted a piece of the dog that bit him. He played a much better game and held the visitors to 6 hits and only 1 run in 9 innings. It was good enough for a 2-1 win. After being released by Bellevue for not playing that well and his poor performance in the game the previous day this had to be a huge mental win for Joe.

Getting back in his groove Joe took on the North Side Board of Trade at home on the 8th of August. Pitching all 9 innings he held the visitors to 2 runs in a 7-2 win. Throwing 2 strikeouts he also had 2 hits in the game.

It was getting into playoff time on the 22nd of August when the Elks played the North Side Board of Trade in the 3rd round of elimination in the Triple-A District and National Baseball Federation Championship. Last year in this round they were knocked off by the Harmarville Consumers. But the Elks were hot today and so was Joe Semler. Lefty Drugmond started the game but after giving up 2 runs in the 5th inning he was pulled and Joe was brought in with 2 men on base and only 1 out. Joe stopped the Traders dead in their tracks and got the Elks out of the inning without any further damage. He went on to hold the Traders scoreless, fanning 5, and held on to a 3-2 win.

Continuing to play regular season games the Elks played the Beaver Independents on the 27th at home. Joe went all 9 innings and even hit a home run over the middle field fence in the 4th inning driving in his 3rd baseman Dewey McGinley. His pitching arm was red hot along with his bat and he held the visitors to 5 hits and struck out 7 in the 3-2 win.

On the 1st of September the Elks traveled to play National Tube at Cycler Park. Joe went all 9 innings and striking out three. The Elks were leading 2-1 heading into the bottom of the 9th inning when Joe let the home team sneak past him with 2 runs for the 3-2 loss.

Playing at home on the 5th against Bellevue the game turned into a home run derby as Bellevue had 2 and the Elks smashed 3. The Elks were up 7-4 going into the 8th inning when Bellevue scored 5 runs. The Elks tried to cool the Bellevue bats by rotating in pitchers but it wasn't enough. Picking up 1 run in the bottom of the 9th inning the Elks fell short and lost 9-8. Lefty Drugmond started for the Elks, Berry came in for a few innings, and Joe closed the loss.

It was back to the National Baseball Federation Championship semi-finals against Homewood on the 12th. Playing at home a huge thunderstorm blew through just before the game making the field slow and soggy. Lefty Drugmond got the start for the Elks and Carl Stewart for Homewood. It was a 1-1 game going into the bottom of the 3rd when Stewart gave up 3 runs. He was relieved by Charley Rohleder the ace who left the Elks back in early July. Rohleder didn't fare much better and gave up 2 more runs before getting out of the inning. Drugmond immediately gave up 3 sharp singles to start the top of the 4th inning. With the bases loaded and no outs Joe Semler was called to the mound. He escaped the inning giving up only 1 run. With Homewood at bat in the top of the 8th inning they had a man on 2nd base and two outs against them. Another storm blew in and the game was halted due to more rain. After waiting 30 minutes it didn't let up and the game was called, 7-5 in favor of the Elks and they were off to the District finals!

The picture on the following page is the Beaver Falls Elks team just before they played West Newton in the Triple-A District Championship Game. Back row left to right: Ed Harvey (manager), Uchrinsko, Gables, Croud, Drugmond, McGinley, Mills, and J.J. Harvey (scorer). Front row left to right: Kelly (captain), Semler, Steiveson, Harvey Jr. (mascot), McKinley,

Young, and Weimer. Joe Semler is also picture pitching to the far right.

Elks team before Championship game[16]

The biggest game of the year came on the 17th of September when the Elks faced West Newton for the Triple-A District title and advancement onto the National Baseball Federation Championship. "Bugs" Hershe got the start for West Newton and Joe got the start for the Elks. West Newton's left fielder Atchinson took Joe long in the 2nd inning for a solo homer. This might have shaken Joe a bit because he gave up 4 runs in the following inning making it a 5-0 game. The Elks looked like they were about to make a comeback in the 4th inning. With the bases load and with 2 outs Joe Semler came to the plate. As the two pitchers faced off in a tense exchange Joe went down swinging and Hershe escaped the inning. The Elks came alive in the 5th inning and there was a close play at the plate when Eddie Kelly gave West Newton's catcher Carl Jorden a deep gash from his spikes in a play called safe. This about cleared the benches in a slugging match. And after all the hoopla the Elks had scored 3 runs to close the gap to 5-3. Feeling a rally West Newton yanked their starter Hershe and replaced him with ace Abe Martin. The Elks almost tied the game in the 6th inning when Steiveson cranked one deep into left field. But the left fielder made a leaping catch to keep it out of the bleachers. Joe gave up another run in the 7th inning to make it 6-3 and Martin kept the Elks scoreless for the 6-3 West Newton win.

Of course, what would a championship game be without a protest and the Elks challenged the eligibility of West Newton's pitcher and 1st baseman. The protest didn't amount to anything and West Newton was declared the winner. Joe only gave up 8 hits but they came at crucial moments and allowed West Newton to score on them. The Elks were held to only 5 hits but managed 3 runs and all three pitchers racked up 3 strikeouts apiece.

Joe wasn't the only Semler to make the National Baseball Federation Championships. Playing in the single-A division District Championship was his bother Al "Curly" Semler a utility ballplayer for Stowe. Unfortunately, they also were beat 5-4 by the Universal Portland Cement team. Single-A ball was pretty popular and their game drew 2,500 fans.

Al had been slowly making his way up through the ranks playing for the Mt. Washington K.O.K.A and then moving over to the McKees Rocks Furniture team. From there he went on to single-A ball with Sto-Rox and now with Stowe. He could play just about anywhere but mostly played shortstop, 2nd base, and the outfield.

Al "Curly" Semler 1926[17]

1926:

The Beaver Falls Elks announced in late February that they had decided to shift over to the Ohio & Pennsylvania League, known as O&P League, for the 1926 season. It had an estimated fan base of over a million and a half people and featured teams such as New Castle, Erie, Youngstown, Akron, Canton, Massillon, and Cleveland.

The starting lineup would be Ziggy Walsh catching, Earl "Chick" Croud 1st base, Tommy Young 2nd base, Bunny Bluffington shortstop, Dewey McGinley 3rd base, Mickey McBride left field, Eddie Kelly middle field, and Lefty Hughes right field. Pitching would be Joe Semler, Jack Ripper, Hildreth, and Towell.

Eddie Kelly turned down a $350 a month contract to play for Nashville in the minor leagues Southern Association. Lefty Drugmond signed a deal with the minor league club Uniontown and Jimmy Uchrinsko went on to play the year in the major leagues for the Washington Senators.

Getting his first start at home on the 1st of May Joe and the Elks hammered General Tires of Youngtown in their season opener. Joe showed the new pitchers on the squad how it was done in a 10-4 win. He even scored 2 runs himself and struck out 2. The Elks bats were on fire as they went through 3 Youngstown pitchers getting 13 hits in the game.

Taking on the Massillon Agathons at home on the 15th Joe got the start. But the Agathons whittled away at Joe for a 5-0 lead by the top of the 4th inning and Jack Ripper came in relief. Eddie Kelly closed the gap in the bottom of the 4th with a 2 run homer making it 5-2. But it wasn't enough and Massillon won 7-3.

The Elks hosted the Erie Sailors on the 22nd and Jack Ripper got the start. He held Erie to 3 hits and 2 runs going into the top of the 8th inning. But with the bases loaded and no outs he injured his arm delivering a pitch. Joe came in and managed to get the side out and only gave up a run to make it 3-2 for Erie. The bats came alive for the Elks in the bottom of the 8th inning and they scored 3 runs turning the tide to 5-3 Elks. Joe held Erie scoreless in the top of the 9th inning for the 5-3 win.

Jack Ripper must not have hurt his arm that bad because he continues to play through the rest of the month. The Elks also bring pitchers Johnny Pearson back, pick up Elvin "Big Ed" Hilty, and Hollis Cannon. So, Joe sees limited action.

He did come in relief of Jack Ripper on the 11th of June against the Homestead Grays. Playing at home Ripper got the start but after only going 2-2/3 innings he was down 8-1 so Joe came in relief. Joe held the Grays to 3 runs for the remainder of the game but the damage was too much for the Elks to overcome and they lost 11-2.

It was a big day along with a large fan turnout when the major league Cincinnati Reds made an exhibition appearance in Beaver Falls on the 24th of June. Joe got the start for the Elks and Artie Nehf for the Reds. The Reds got to Joe in the 2nd inning for 3 hits and scored 2 runs pulling ahead 2-1. The game then went scoreless until the 6th inning when the Reds added another run winning it 3-1. Joe held his own against the major leaguers giving up 9 hits and fanning 4. Nehf had 6 hits against him and fanned 6.

By the 26th Jack Ripper and Ed Hilty had been workhorses on the mound and Hilty alone had racked up 6 straight wins since joining the club earlier in the month. Just an interesting note on the game Ed Hitly got his 6th straight win. It was against

Erie on the 26th and Weber, the starting pitcher for Erie, was ejected from the game for roughing up the ball with emery cloth. It was also Booster Day for the Elks and one lucky fan drove away in a brand new Studebaker automobile!

The following day Joe got the start against the Erie Sailors and Weber, who was ejected the previous day, started for Erie. Joe was up 3-0 going into the bottom of the 8th inning when Erie smacked a couple of singles off of him. Jack Ripper came in relief giving up a run, but it was enough to secure the 3-1 Elk win.

If you remember in the introduction of this book, I mentioned that Joe was offered contracts with the Cincinnati Reds on a couple of occasions. After this game with Erie a scout with the Reds came up to Joe and asked him to sign with them. Joe asked how much he was offering and the scout said $500 a month. Joe turned him down. Later in life he said it was a mistake to have turned him down, but at the time he thought he should have been offered more money to play in the major leagues. Joe said he was making just about that much with the Elks and his carpentry. He was making $200 a month with the Elks and around $250 as a carpenter. And I'm sure there were perks playing for the Elks and pitching jobs on the side. Plus, with the Elks he still had his carpentry income, which he would have to give up if he went to the major leagues. He said that scout for the Reds made that offer to him three times that year, and he turned him down each time.[47]

To close out the month Joe got the start at home against New Castle. He was up 4-3 going into the top of the 9th inning. After giving up a run to tie the game 4-4 and putting 2 men on base Ed Hilty was brought in relief. He managed to get out of the inning and held New Castle scoreless until the top of the 12th inning when New Castle scored a run to make it 5-4. But the Elks bats came alive in the bottom of the 12th to score 2 runs for the win and to give Ed Hilty his 7th straight victory.

It was a disappointing July 5th in front of their home fans when the Elks got swept in a double header against the Cleveland Tellings. Johnny Pearson started the morning game and didn't get much defensive support in his 4-2 loss. Joe had the afternoon game which went for a long 12 innings. Tellings scored first in the bottom of the 4th inning and the Elks tied it up in the top of the 8th inning. Joe stayed in the game and Tellings finally got to him again in the bottom of the 12th inning scoring a run and winning the game 2-1.

Travelling to Akron to play the General Tire club on the 11th Joe was facing a red hot team who had won their past 16 games. The Elks were up 5-0 and Joe had plenty of breathing room. But he started to get a bit shaky in the 3rd inning and gave up 4 runs whittling his lead down to 5-4. He settled down after that and held Akron scoreless for the remainder of the game. The Elks added another run to make it a 6-4 win.

The Akron boys got their revenge when Joe and the Elks returned on the 25th. Pitching all 9 innings Joe never got ahead of the General Tire club and fell to them 7-2.

August started out with the release of Jack Ripper. The Elks had to trim their salary and decided to release Ripper, who was actually pitching well. The Elks stuck with Joe Semler, Elvin Hilty, Johnny Pearson, and Hollis Cannon as their pitchers. Pearson and Cannon were also good utility players which probably kept them over Ripper. Unlike Joe and Ed Hilty guys like Johnny Pearson and Hollis Cannon played just about every game either in the infield or outfield when they were not pitching. Joe and Ed Hilty strictly pitched. Occasionally Joe would play 1st base or the outfield, but it was rare. It didn't take Ripper long to find a home and he joined rival Youngstown immediately.

There wasn't any time to dwell on losing Ripper as the Elks traveled to Massillon Ohio to play the Agathons on the 1st of August. The home team was putting their young southpaw hurler Edgar Gilliland up against veteran Joe Semler. The Agathons jumped out ahead 1-0 in the 3rd inning and then it was 2-1 after 6 innings. The Agathons got 1 more run in the 8th for the 3-1 win.

Joe started at home against Jewey Coen and New Castle on the 4th. Proving that he was worth keeping Joe held the visitors to 1 hit and fanned 5. Coen was also pitching an excellent game as well and only had given up 2 hits and struck out 4. The pitching duel ended in a 0-0 tie after being called by rain in the 7th inning.

It was a tougher day against Erie three days later on the 8th. Joe was starting against former Boston Red Sox major leaguer

Hugh Bediant. After falling behind 7-4 in 3-1/2 innings Johnny Pearson came in relief. But he couldn't do much better against the Sailors bats and the Elks fell 13-5.

It was a record setting double header for the Canton Hooper Coal team when their ace pitcher Glenn Shinn tossed both the morning and afternoon games for wins. Hollis Cannon got the start for the Elks in the morning game and after giving up 2 runs in the 3rd inning Joe came in relief. He pitched the remainder of the game giving up 1 more run in the 3-1 loss. Carl Stewart started the afternoon game for the Elks and lasted until the 5th inning when he gave up 7 runs and was relieved by Joe. He gave up 2 more runs and the Elks got swept 9-5.

At home against Canton on the 21st Joe pitched all 9 innings in a spectacular 4-3 win. Down 3-0 going into the 6th inning Joe held the visitors scoreless for the remainder of the game. This gave the Elks bats time to rally for 4 runs and the win.

New Castle came to Beaver Falls on the 25th and it was another nail biter. The Elks jumped out to a 2-0 lead in the 1st inning. By the 5th inning they were up to 3-0 and Joe, who was pitching, was cruising along. New Castle rallied in the top of the 7th inning scoring 2 runs to make it 3-2. In the top of 8th inning it looked like New Castle might tie the game when they had Buzzard on 3rd base and McCullough on 1st base. McCullough went to steal 2nd base and the Elks catcher Musser bluffed the throw to 2nd and snapped it instead to Dewey McGinley at 3rd who tagged out Buzzard standing off the bag. That retired the side and allowed the 3-2 Elk win.

It was almost brother against brother when the Elks traveled to the Stowe grounds to play Al "Curly" Semler and his Stowe Independents. Hollis Cannon got the start for the Elks and he easily handled Stowe 5-0. Joe sat in the dugout and watched his brother Al, who was Stowe's team captain, play middle field. Unfortunately, he didn't see Al do much as he went hitless.

Even though Stowe was a Single-A team they ranked very high in that division and played Triple-A teams in the area such as the Elks, Bellevue, and the Homestead Grays to name a few. The games didn't count for anything more than exhibition but they drew in big crowds, which drew in money.

Hosting the Cleveland Tellings on the 28th of August Joe got the start in the morning game of a double header. The Elks catcher Messer hit a homer in the 3rd inning to make the game 1-0. In the 8th inning the Elks Lefty Hughes was hit by a pitch and Ed Kelly, Dewy McGinley, Johnny Pearson, and Bunny Bluffington all laid down bunts driving in 3 runs. Another run on an error in the 8th inning and a run in the 9th inning sealed up a 5-0 win and shutout for Joe. In the afternoon game the Elks started a young kid by the name of Church from Midland, PA. He held Cleveland to 3 runs in a 5-3 win and all important sweep for the Elks.

It was very common to bunt against a non-fielding pitcher in these days and teams would do it as long as they could. There was a lengthy article about this in one of the Pittsburgh papers in the beginning of the year and Joe Semler was mentioned as being one of very few fielding pitchers that this bunting technique wouldn't work against.

Playing Bellevue in the North Borough to close out August Joe pitched against Joe Miller in a 7 inning game. The Elks scored 2 runs in the top of the 3rd inning and Bellevue answered with 2 of their own in the bottom of the 3rd to tie the game 2-2. It happened again in the top of the 5th inning when the Elks scored a run and Bellevue answered with a run in the bottom of the 5th which tied it up 3-3. In the top of the 7th inning the Elks scored 3 runs. Joe held them scoreless in the bottom of the 7th inning for a 6-3 win.

In an interesting game on the 6th of September against New Castle Joe started the game pitching against their hurler Rodenbaugh. But after the Elks scored 3 runs off of him in the 1st inning their 45 year old manager Bill Steen came in relief! That seemed to cool the Elks bats and they only scored 1 more run in the game. Joe gave up 3 runs in the 4th inning, 1 in the 7th inning, and 1 in the 9th inning for the 5-4 loss.

If the game on the 6th wasn't interesting enough this game on the 11th to close out the regular season had that one beat. The Elks were playing a hand-picked team from the Beaver County Industrial league, dubbed the All-Stars. Johnny Pearson pitched the game for the Elks. Comfortably ahead 10-4 going into the 8th inning the Elks decided to have some fun with the home town crowd and Joe Semler came in to play 1st base and Dewey McGinley at 3rd base and Hollis Cannon in left field swapped position. This seemed to amuse the fans! The Elks played the last two innings this way and easily won 12-6.

Johnny Pearson is an interesting fellow. If you remember he was the "iron man" that pitched both games of that double header sweep against Cleveland in the National Baseball Federation Championship back in 1922, the last time the Elks were World Champions. He was a fantastic athlete and over the years was offered contracts by major league teams like the Pittsburgh Pirates, Philadelphia Phillies and Detroit Tigers, all of which he turned down. It was said that his only drawback was that sometimes he was hard to handle. For instance, one time he was playing against Wheeling and he pitched a shutout game for 8 innings. Instead of returning to the mound for the 9th inning he just walked out of the park and left his team to close the game because he felt that they were not providing him any run support. And again in Sharon he had pitched a 9 inning shutout against the Sharon Elks and the game was tied 0-0 and went into extra innings. When asked to pitch the extra innings he refused. When he was ordered out to the mound he proceeded to intentionally walk the next 4 batters so the opposing team won! He has bounced around with several teams over the years but seems to always come back to the Elks. And with the Elks he has not only been an excellent pitcher but also an exceptional utility man.

It was back home to old Olympia Park for Joe when he started the game against the Washington Heights Traders. It was a pitching duel in the 5 inning exhibition game that ended in a 1-1 tie.

Joe Semler August 1926[18]

There was no playoffs for the Elks this year. They settled for playing a double header against the Homestead Grays at Forbes Field on the 18th of September. The season didn't end on a winning note and the Elks got swept. In the morning game Hollis Cannon pitched against George Britt. The game went back and forth until the Grays pulled ahead in the 8th inning for an 8-5 win. The afternoon game had Joe pitted up against Oscar Owen. The Grays jumped out early and never looked back. Owen only allowed 2 hits and fanned 11 Elks in his 9-3 win.

The O&P League published their All-Star team for the year. It wasn't a team that would actually play, but who they deemed were the best players in the league. The Elks had three players make the team - Ed Hilty was selected as one of the two pitchers, Romele as the 2nd baseman, and Eddie Kelly in middle field. Kelly also led the league in homeruns with 11. Joe Semler got an honorable pitcher mention.[21]

Al Semler and the Stowe Independents finished well and took the Single-A district championship title again. They went off to play in the National Baseball Federation Single-A Championship but were defeated in the final rounds.

1927:

The year started out with this printed in the January 16th edition of the Pittsburgh Press;

*"LOCAL SEMI-PRO POW-WOW ----Whether it was a "pow-wow" or "stove-league" session there was baseball chatte*r

from years ago to the present at the party recently at Joe Semler's home where Harry Powell brought together such luminaries as Eddie Kelly, Tommy Young, Leo Mackey, Sam Griffith, Elmer Yoder, Wally Wickline, William Geer and Al Semler for a good time. Who said it's winter time?"

You know you're becoming popular when you make the gossip section of the city paper! Most of those listed at the party were semi-pro players like Joe, with the exception of Elmer Yoder (Yoter) who was currently playing 3rd base in the major leagues for the Chicago Cubs. He had attended High School and played semi-pro ball in McKees Rocks and was friends with Joe. Elmer played and coached in the minor and major leagues into the 1960's.

Leo Mackey was a minor league catcher from the area who in 1926 and 27 was playing for Nashville in the Southern League. Like Elmer he would occasionally play with Joe on exhibition teams when they were in town.

Eddie Kelly had been a long time teammate of Joe's and Eddie had been with the Elks since 1920. He also started out playing at Olympia Park for the Mt. Washington K.O.K.A a few years earlier than Joe, in 1917. He had numerous offers to play in the minor and major leagues but continues to turn them down. He said he liked playing for the Elks and felt he played his best baseball with them.

Wally Wickline was a teammate and manager of Al's and William Geer a manager/owner of the Stowe ball club. After winning the District Single-A Championship last year the papers were reporting in the spring that they might be stepping it up to Triple-A this year. There was even talk of Joe Semler pitching some of their games for them since they were in different leagues, Stowe in the Alleghany County League and the Elks in the O&P League. You never know, maybe that was the hot topic at the pow-wow party…

By April Ed Harvey had signed and announced his lineup for the year which consisted of James Smith catching, Joe Semler, Ed Hilty, and Ray Bond pitching, Earl Croud on 1st base, Andy Swetonic on 2nd base, Hartzell at shortstop, Dewey McGinley at 3rd base, and Eddie Kelly, Johnny Pearson and Lefty Hughes in the outfield.

It was an opening day barn burner on the 30th of April at Beaver Falls when the Elks hosted the Cleveland Tellings. Ed Hilty started for the Elks and was ahead 3-0 after 3 innings. Ed sprained his ankle sliding into 3rd base in the bottom of the 3rd inning and was relieved by Ray Bond to start the 4th inning. Cleveland jumped on Ray for 4 runs to tie the game 4-4. Each team scored in the 5th inning to make it 5-5. The Elks jumped ahead in the 6th inning scoring 2 more runs and in the 8th inning 1 more run to take an 8-5 lead. In the top of the 9th inning Bond had loaded the bases and Joe Semler was brought in. He pitched his way out of the jam and the Elks won 8-5 Elk.

The next day Joe got his start on the road against the Erie Sailors. In front of 1,500 Sailor fans Joe got behind in the 1st inning but after that it was smooth sailing to a 10-6 win. He pitched all 9 innings and had 4 strikeouts.

It finally happened on the 5th of May when Joe and Al played in the same game and on the same team! They were playing on the Stowe team with Al in middle field and Joe pitching. It was against the North Side Traders who had their own brothers playing – Art, Dan, and Jim Rooney. Art and Dan would go on to form and own the Pittsburgh Steelers football team in 1933. The game started with Al in middle field and Nifty Gardner pitching for Stowe. After 3 innings the game was tied 1-1. The Traders then scored 1 run in the 4th inning and 3 runs in the 5th inning to make it 5-1. Stowe came back in the 6th inning and scored 3 runs and 1 more in the 7th inning to tie it up 5-5. In the top of the 8th inning the Traders had men on 2nd and 3rd base with no outs. Gardner was yanked and Joe came in relief. He struck out the next 2 batters and the umpire called the game due to darkness. Al went hitless and Dan Rooney hit a homer off of Gardner.

As I was growing up I always noticed that there was a Christmas card from the Pittsburgh Steelers signed by the Rooney's on display at Joe's house around the holidays. I thought it was really cool but I never really knew the connection between them and my grandfather. Now it all makes sense, they played baseball together.

At Home taking on the Butler Bruinoils on the 21st Joe took the mound. The Bruinoils jumped out in the top of the 3rd inning 1-0. They then picked up 4 more runs in the top of the 5th inning to make it 5-0. The Elks bats came alive in the bottom of the 5th when Eddie Kelly hit a homer with 2 men on to make it a 5-3 game. Picking up another run in the top of the 7th

inning Butler made it a 6-3 game. The Elks answered with 3 more runs in the bottom of the 7th inning to tie things up at 6-6. In the bottom of the 8th inning Joe got on first through a fielder's choice. He advanced to 2nd base on a wild pitch and then scored on a Johnny Pearson single making it 7-6. Joe took the mound and blanked the Bruinoils in the top of the 9th inning to secure the win. He had 6 strikeouts, the win put them at 5-0 in the O&P League, and in first place.

The Semler brothers got together against Homewood on the 2nd of June. Joe took the mound and Al middle field. Joe wasn't the only Elk wearing a Stowe uniform. Tommy Young was playing 2nd base and Dewey McGinley playing 3rd. Stowe jumped out to a 2-0 lead in the bottom of the 1st inning. Homewood picked a run up in the top of the 4th inning but McGinley hit a solo homer in the bottom of the 4th to make it 3-1. Joe pitched 6 strikeouts and got the 3-1 win. Although Al was hitless in the game, he wasn't doing too bad this year and was hitting .261. Stowe really needed the assistance of the Elks players. They were 0-4 and in last place in the Alleghany County League going into this game.

Back in an Elks uniform Joe got the start against Bellevue in the North Borough on the 7th. The game was tied up 3-3 after 6 innings. The Elks scored 1 run in the top of the 7th inning to make it 4-3, but Bellevue answered in the bottom of the 7th with 2 runs to make it 5-4. Joe was relieved by Johnny Pearson and both teams were quiet in the 8th inning. The Elks scored 3 runs in the top of the 9th inning jumping ahead making it 7-5.

Bellevue squeezed out one more run in the bottom of the 9th but it wasn't enough of a rally and the Elks won 7-6.

In a Friday night game on the 10th the Stowe Independents, who were on a winning streak, hosted the Beaver Falls Elks. The Semler brothers faced off and Al was in middle field for Stowe and strangely Joe was in right field for the Elks. The Elks rotated in three pitchers during the game- Lefty Hughes, Johnny Pearson, and newly acquired Red Whitmore. It was a tight game that went back and forth until the Elks pulled ahead in the bottom of the 8th inning winning the game 5-4. Al had a hit and drove in a run and Joe was hitless.

On the 12th up in Erie the Elks took on the Sailors at Pennsylvania Railroad Field. Joe got the start and kept the Sailors scoreless for the first 5 innings while the Elks jumped out to a 6-0 lead. The Sailors picked up 2 runs in the bottom of the 6th inning to close the gap to 6-2. Then in the bottom of the 8th inning Joe let them score 4 more runs to tie things up at 6-6. Red Whitmore came in relief and held the Sailors in the 9th inning. The game went into the 10th inning and the Elks scored a run in the top of that inning making it 7-6. Whitmore held the Sailors in the bottom of the 10th for a 7-6 win. Joe struck out 6, had 2 hits – one for a double, and drove in a run.

Two days later at home Joe got another chance at the Sailors. The game turned into a pitching duel between Joe and Jimmy Sykes of Erie. Joe gave up only 4 hits and Jimmy 5 hits. The game went scoreless until the bottom of the 9th inning when Eddie Kelly doubled to left field. Lefty Hughes hit a hard single into middle field allowing Kelly to score from 2nd base ending the game 1-0.

It was a rough Thursday night game for Joe, Al, and the Stowe Independents on the 23rd. They were in 6th place in their league with a record of 4-9 and needed a win. Joe got the start against McKeesport and was backed up with a few Elks like Dewey McGinley on 3rd base and Eddie Kelly in middle field. Things looked great with Stowe up 4-0 going into the bottom of the 7th inning. Then McKeesport scored 1 run in the bottom of the 7th inning making it 4-1. In the bottom of the 8th inning Joe fell apart and gave up 5 runs to make it 6-4 and a Stowe loss. The loss placed Stowe in second to last place at 4-10. Al had a good game with 3 hits and Joe just as well with 2 hits, one being a homer, and 4 strikeouts. But of course he did get the loss for the game.

Joe had a better day two days later pitching at home against the Butler Bruinoils. Shutting out Butler 8-0 he had a commanding day on the mound. He also helped himself offensively with a hit and driving in a run. The win placed them at 17-1 in the O&P League and well ahead of 2nd place Massillon who were 12-6.

The next day the Elks had a double header against the 2nd place Agathons in Massillon, Ohio. Red Whitamore opened the morning game and it was the Agathons ahead for the entire game. The Elks almost came back in the top of the 9th inning but fell short 6-5. Ed Hilty started the afternoon game and it was a close one. Joe came in and played left field in the later part of the game so Johnny Pearson could move to 3rd base. In the end Ed Hilty got his 7th win in a row with a 7-6 victory.

Trying to get Stowe back to a winning record their owner signed even more Elk players to try and bolster his team. Of course the Elks first obligation was to play for their own team but were used by Stowe whenever possible. Well the plan backfired against Homewood on the 28th. Stowe got blown out 29-8. No that's not a typo, Homewood scored 29 runs! Stowe had started their own pitcher by the name of VanHorn. Then they brought in Dewey McGinley from 3rd base to try his arm. When that didn't work, they tried Joe who was playing left field. Nothing could stop Homewood and Stowe's record went to 5-13. Joe went hitless and Al didn't play.

It didn't get any better for Joe the next day against New Castle back in the O&P League. Joe got the start on the road against New Castles "Lefty" Feigert. I find it humorous that everyone who throws left handed back then automatically got the first name "Lefty." Well, "Lefty" was an ace who had tried out for the major leagues. He didn't leave any doubt as to his ability when he beat the Elks 6-1 and handing them only their 3rd loss of the year. Joe got banged up for 11 hits and only 3 strikeouts.

The Elks secured 1st place in the first half of the O&P League's season by beating New Castle at home on July the 2nd. Ed Hitly got the start and Joe played 1st base for the first few innings. After the 1st inning the Elks were up 1-0. In the bottom of the 2nd inning Joe got on with a force and then Johnny Pearson hit a homer and brought them both around for the 3-0 final score. Ed Hilty got his 8th straight win and moved the Elks to 18-3.

On the road in Cleveland Joe didn't fare as well as Ed the previous day. Starting against the Tellings Joe and the Elks jumped out to a 1-0 lead in the 1st inning. Tellings made it 2-1 in the 3rd inning and it went to 3-2 in the 6th. By the top of the 8th inning it was tied up 3-3. But Joe couldn't slow the Telling's bats and they picked up 2 runs in the bottom of the 8th to make it 5-3 and the final score. That brought the Elks to 18-4.

Traveling to Canton, Ohio to play Canton on the 10th of July Joe got the start. He couldn't get any momentum going and Canton stayed ahead of the Elks the entire game. Even a triple from Joe couldn't help him offensively and they lost 7-6. The loss made them 1-1 in the seasons 2nd half O&P League standings.

Joe finally got a good win by pitching a fine game against the Havana Red Sox. Pitching at home on the 12th he held the Red Sox scoreless until the top of the 5th inning when they scored a run cutting the Elks led to 2-1. They tied the game up in the top of the 6th inning but the Elks answered them in the bottom of the inning with 2 runs making it 4-2. Picking up 4 more runs in the bottom of the 7th inning sealed the deal at 8-2. Joe fanned 8, had 2 hits – one being a double, and drove in a run.

It was a fan pleaser in New Castle when Joe took the mound as the Elks rolled into town on the 16th. Joe started and *"had a wide breaking curve working to perfection."*[22] The game was tied 2-2 going into the bottom of the 8th inning when New Castle scored 2 runs making it 4-2. The Elks bats couldn't do anything in the top of the 9th inning and that's how it ended. Joe fanned 6, hit a triple, and drove in a run. This brought the Elks to 2-2 in the O&P Leagues 2nd half of the season. Joe was currently 6-3, Ed Hilty was 9-0, Red Whitmore 4-0, Johnny Pearson 1-0, and Ray Bond was 3-1.

August rolls in with a shakeup in the Stowe Independents club. Bill Geer the owner/manager was going to disband the team due to a poor season, but Wally Wickline agreed to manage the team with the assistance of Al Semler. The Elks were also struggling after coming in 1st in the opening half of the season and were now in 4th place in the O&P League in the 2nd half of the season. To hopefully win some more games the Elks signed a hot hurler by the name of Andy Hospidor to hopefully help them out.

Trying to gain some momentum the Elks traveled to Erie on the 7th of August to play the Sailors in a double header. This should have been easy pickings for the Elks because the Sailors were only 2-6 in the second half of the season. Well Joe took the mound in the morning game and things looked promising as they jumped out to a 3 run lead. But Joe slowly let them come back and Erie beat them 4-3. Things didn't get much better in the second game. Their new pitcher Andy Hospidor started the afternoon game and it was a 3-3 tie after 3 innings. Then Erie jumped ahead 6-3 in the bottom of the 4th inning. Andy Hospidor was up at bat in the top of the 5th inning and got into an argument with the umpire on a called strike. After using a lot of profanity he was tossed from the game. The Elks in protest threatened to pull out of the game, but decided against it because they would have forfeited the game. The Elks tied the game in the top of the 6th inning at 6-6 where it stayed, until the 10th inning when the umpired called it so the Elks could catch their train home!

Trying to help Stowe get out of their funk Joe pitched on the 12th for them in a Friday night game against the Northside Civics. It turned into a pitching battle between Joe and the Civics pitcher Heidler. The game was decided in the top of the 9th inning when the Civics got a run off of Joe and won 1-0. Joe allowed 6 hits and Heidler 3 hits. Al didn't play.

Getting his next start for the Elks on the 15th Joe went up against the Beltzhoover club at Mckinley Park. The Elks jumped out to a 3 run lead in the top of the 3rd inning but Beltzhoover answered back with 5 runs in the bottom of the 3rd inning. Joe gave up 2 more runs in the bottom of the 4th inning to make it a 7-3 game. Johnny Pearson swapped positions with Joe in left field and held Beltzhoover to only 1 more run while the Elks bats came alive to win the game 9-8.

Playing Elwood City on the 18th in a Saturday night game the Elks threw a strange armada of pitchers at Elwood City for no apparent reason but to possibly give them a workout. Dewey McGinley pitched a few innings while Johnny Pearson played 3rd base. Then they swapped spots so Pearson could pitch a few innings. Then Hartzell came to the mound from 1st base to pitch and was replaced by Fritz at 1st base. All the while Joe played right field. The unorthodox pitching worked and the Elks won 7-3 and moved to 6-6 in the league standings.

At home against the Beaver Grays on the 23rd Joe got the start. He got rocked for 4 runs in the top of the 3rd inning and 3 more in the 4th inning. Down 7-0 he was relieved by Andy Hospidor. With the bases loaded in the bottom of the 5th inning Eddie Kelly sent one over the left field fence for a grand slam making it a 7-4 game. In the bottom of the 7th inning Hospidor was running out a base hit and collided with the Grays 1st baseman and injured his ankle. The game was then called due to darkness and the Grays won 7-4.

The following evening the Elks played the North Side Board of Trade at Saltworks Field. Joe started for the Elks, Al Semler was playing middle field, and Dan Rooney 1st base for the Traders. It was a 3-3 tie after the 2nd inning, then the Traders picked up 3 more runs in the bottom of the 4th inning to make it 6-3. The game was set at only 6 innings and that's how it ended, 6-3 for the Traders. Joe had 5 strikeouts and Al drove in a run.

In a Saturday game on the 27th the Elks hosted the Akron General Tires. Johnny Pearson got the start for the Elks and held General Tire scoreless with only 2 hits after 6 innings. With a 7-0 lead he handed it off to Joe to take it home. Joe only gave up 1 hit and kept it scoreless for the remaining 3 innings for a 7-0 Elk win.

Beaver Falls Elks August 1927[23]

The picture above is left to right: Joe Semler, Harzell, Dewey McGinley, Eddie Kelly, Johnny Pearson, and Lefty Hughes.

As the season was winding down the O&P League was under financial stress and was about to disband. Teams were finding it hard to pay players and make enough in gate revenue to make a profit. The Elks in fact hadn't played an O&P League opponent in a week. At this point they didn't know if there would even be a playoff series to finish up the season. But this was common baseball in these days, leagues and teams were constantly starting and folding. To add to things the Elks released Andy Hospidor.

Playing Beltzhoover again on the 1st of September for a 7 inning game they met at the Warrington Park Grounds. Joe and Johnny Pearson shared the pitching duties in a game that had the Elks up 6-3 after 4 innings. But Beltzhoover tied it up at 6-6 after 6 innings. The Elks scored 2 runs in the top of the 7th inning and Beltzhoover only answered with 1 run in the bottom of the 7th for an 8-7 Elk win.

Two days later in Beaver Falls Joe took on Beltzhoover again. In one of his best games of the year he fanned 7 and held the visitors to only 1 run in a 2-1 Elk victory. The game was scoreless until Beltzhoover took a 1-0 lead in the top of the 6th inning. The Elks bats had been quiet but finally came alive in the bottom of the 8th inning to score 2 runs. That was enough to secure the 2-1 win.

The following day the Elks traveled to Akron to play the General Tires. Joe played 1st base and Hartzell pitched for the Elks in a game that was tied 5 times and had 6 stolen bases. Finally in the bottom of the 10th inning the General Tires scored a run for a 5-4 win.

The Homestead Grays came to Beaver Falls for a double header on the 10th of September. Ed Hilty got the pitching start and Al Semler played middle field in the morning game. In probably Ed Hilty's worst game of the year he got rocked for 12 runs and 4 homers in a 12-3 beating. Al was hitless. Thankfully rain moved in and cancelled the afternoon game.

And that's how the season ended. There were no playoffs for several reasons. First the O&P League was struggling and it was every team for themselves. The Elks who had won the 1st half of the season and Massillon who had won the second half in the O&P League had arranged to play a championship series but it fell through.

1928:

The pre-season started out as usual with a lot of posturing by the area teams as leagues were formed and players were signed. It appeared as if the Elks would be playing back in the O&P League as it seemed to have formed back up. Probably the biggest roster changes with the Elks was Ed Hilty and Eddie Kelly. Both were lured away with big contract offers. Granted Hilty was the best pitcher in the O&P League last year and was now using that leverage for a better contract. But he went to play for Bellevue so the Elks would be facing him. Eddie Kelly had always been an outstanding player and the team's captain. His signing with Beltzhoover would also be tough on the Elks. But if it was any consolation the Elks picked up Walt Gibson who played for Beltzhoover last year and was a great lead-off man who batted .377.

Joe got the start in the home opener against the Akron General Tires on the 5th of May. Joining him on the field was only one former teammate from last year – Dewey McGinley at 3rd base. The Elks jumped out ahead 2-0 in the bottom of the 1st inning. Akron answered with 2 runs of their own in the top of the 2nd inning to tie the game. In the top of the 4th they scored 3 more runs to make it a 5-2 game. The Elks replied with a run in the bottom of the 4th inning to close the gap to 5-3. Akron picked up another run in the top of the 8th inning to make it 6-3. Rallying in the bottom of the 9th inning Dewey McGinley drove in 2 runs off of a double to make it 6-5. But his fellow teammates left him stranded and the Elks lost 6-5.

The season had already started for the O&P League but wouldn't start for many other leagues in the area until mid-May. Like last year Joe was going to split his time between other teams when not engaged with the Elks. He would still dabble with Stowe and it was headline news when he signed with the club from Homewood-Brushton who were in the Alleghany County League. Also known as the Dalymen, in a nod to their manager Hank Daly, Homewood had been a strong contender last year but were lacking in the pitching department. Obviously, they were out looking for talent and talked Joe into joining them.

Al Semler was starting the year with the Stowe Civics again, although they had changed the last part of their name from Independents to Civics. They were now playing in the Alleghany City League instead of the County League. The Alleghany County League wasn't supposed to start until May 15th. The day before the season started Dewey McGinley sign with the Beltzhoover club and would split his time with them and the Elks. The Elks signed a 3rd baseman by the name of Heinie Boll to fill in for McGinley since he was currently injured. They also resigned Jim Urinsko, which would be some help after losing Ed Hilty.

Playing an exhibition game against the House of David in Beaver Falls on the 1st of June Foster got the start for the Elks. He held the visitors scoreless until the top of the 5th inning when he gave up 5 runs to close the Elks lead to 1. Joe came in relief and held the visitors scoreless for the remaining 3 innings for a 7-5 Elk win.

The House of David club were a traveling team from Michigan who played anyone they could to make money. They lived in a religious commune and played to support themselves. They were in fact a great team that used players from their own religious community and also hired professional players to make them even better and attract more people to their games. They were noted for playing with long hair and full beards, which was very unconventional at the time and helped draw in crowds.

Joe got the start for the Elks on the 13th of June against the New Castle Cents. Playing at New Castles Centennial Field the Elks scored first but the Cents answered back and the score went back and forth. Finally, the Elks pulled ahead in the 8th inning when their new 3rd baseman Heinie Boll beat out a throw at home when the Cents tried to pick off Frank Weimer stealing 2nd base. With the Elks up 10-7 going into the bottom of the 9th inning the Cents tried to rally. They only managed to muster up 1 more run, but in doing so Joe hit their left fielder, Red Leonard, in the head on a pitched ball. Leonard started towards 1st base and collapsed. He got back up and stumbled to 1st Base where a doctor from the stands came out to check on him and deemed him fit to play. This was way before the days of batting helmets and batters just wore their baseball cap, so they had no head protection. Well, the Elks won the game 10-8 and Joe had his first win of the season.

In an interesting double header against the Homestead Grays on Saturday the 16th newly acquired Jim Urinsko got the start in the first game that started at 3pm and was played on Forbes Field. Jim pitched a pretty nice game against Lefty Williams but lost it 5-2. Joe got the start in the 6:30pm evening game which they played over at Steel Works Park in Duquesne. He was going against the Gray's starter Sam Streeter. Joe stayed ahead of the Grays the entire game and fanned 8 along with 2 hits, one being a double, to beat the Grays 5-2. Joe said that he struck out the Grays big hitters Jasper "Jap" Washington and John Beckwith several times in the game and each time the crowd went wild. He said that they would swing so hard at his pitches that they would just about fall down when they swung and missed the ball.[47]

In a hard fought game in Beaver Falls on the 23rd against Canton, Joe went all 9 innings in a game that went down to the wire. Behind 5-3 going into the bottom of the 9th inning the Elks bats came alive to score 3 runs and to give Joe and the Elks a 6-5 win. Joe had a triple and drove in a run and Johnny Pearson a homer. The Elks were 9-4 in the O&P League and in 3rd place behind Massillon and New Castle. In a bit of sad news Dewey McGinley was released from the Elks roster due to injuries.

Closing out June Joe got the call to start against Akron General Tire at home. Akron started a fella named Vitorella but he was relieved by Walker after hurting his arm. Walker pitched for a while then was relieved by Knell. Veteran hurler Joe stayed in for all 11 innings of this tight one which finally ended with Akron winning 2-1.

Starting the second half of the season clubs were having a tough time getting games in due to the wet weather. Heavy rains in May and June had caused a lot of cancellations and teams were scrambling to get in makeup games. But with limited ball fields and players work schedules this was tough. Teams were also complaining in the paper that they were losing money because without games, there was no revenue. And even when games were played fan turnout was light. Ed Harvey of the Elks even stated that he would stop playing in Youngstown because the ticket sales there had gotten so low. And even though Joe was retained to play for the Homewood club he had yet to pitch a game for them.

Pitching for the Stowe Civics on the 3rd of July Joe started against the Garfield team and their hurler named Stocker. Playing at Stowe Field Joe held the visitors to 5 hits and 3 strikeouts in a 5-0 shutout. Al Semler did not play.

It was a bit tougher on the 7th when the Homestead Grays came to Beaver Falls. Joe started against Sam Streeter in a rematch of their earlier game in June. The Grays were ahead 5-2 going into the 8th inning when Joe was relieved by Red Whitmore. Joe was not only behind but he had been hit hard for 4 homers.

Whitmore held the Grays scoreless in the top of the 9th inning and the Elks did manage a rally but it wasn't enough and lost 5-3.

The Elks on the road squared up against the New Castle Cents on the 8th. Johnny Pearson started for the Elks and had a 3-0 lead, but after letting New Castle tie the game 3-3 in the 6th inning Red Whitmore came in relief. He coasted to a 7-3 lead until the bottom of the 9th inning. New Castle started to rally scoring 2 runs to make it a 7-5 game. Joe came in relief of Whitmore and quieted things down for the 7-5 win.

The Cents traveled to Beaver Falls on the 18th and Joe faced their ace pitcher Jewey Coen. The game was scoreless until the top of the 4th inning when New Castle scored 2 runs. Joe and the Elks just couldn't catch up and the game ended 4-1 in favor of the Cents.

Joe got another chance at the Homestead Grays on the 21st of July in the morning game of a double header. This time he was facing Lefty Williams. The Elks pulled ahead 5-0 at the end of 4 innings with the help of a 3 run homer from the Elks middle fielder Ollie Carnegie. But in the top of the 5th inning "Smokey" Joe Williams came up to bat for Lefty Williams with the bases loaded and cranked out a grand slam home run. Johnny Pearson came in relief of Joe but he couldn't slow the Grays down either and they went on to win the game 8-5. The Elks got revenge in the afternoon game when Jim Urinsko pitched a 4-3 win.

Trying to get a game over on the O&P League leaders the Elks traveled to New Castle to have a go at the Cents on the 28th. Joe was going against former major leaguer Earl Mosely. The Elks as usual jumped out to a 3-0 lead when Ollie Carnegie once again hit a 3 run homer. New Castle tied the game up in the 6th inning on some nifty hits and in the 7th inning scored the go ahead run to make it a 4-3 New Castle win. The 41 year old Mosely fanned 9 and kept the Elks to 5 hits.

Ollie Carnegie who hit those two 3 run homers in the past couple of games was nicknamed the "Bambino" and referred to in the semi-pro world as their version of Babe Ruth. He played in the early 20's then took a break due to health reasons and had just started playing again last year.

Playing Dormont at home on the 5th of August Joe took up a spot on 1st base while Red Whitmore did the pitching. Ollie Carnegie hit a 2 run homer in the 2nd inning to give the Elks a 2-0 lead. Dormont picked up a run in the top of the 4th inning to make it 2-1. Then Red let the visitors score 5 runs in the top of the 7th inning to make it a 6-2 game. The "Bambino" smacked a solo homer in the bottom of the 7th inning to edge the Elks closer but it just wasn't enough and Dormont won 6-3.

Owing to the decline in revenue and fan support the Bellevue club announced it was disbanding and would no longer field a semi-pro team. They said if they did come back next year, it would only be as an amateur team. At the time amateur teams didn't pay their players but they could get a share of any profits made in championship games.

And finally, Joe gets to don a Homewood uniform on the 9th of August against Dormont. He was joined by fellow Elks Ollie Carnegie in middle field and Heinie Boll at 3rd base. Buzz Isherwood got the start for Homewood and was immediately rocked for 5 runs in the top of the 1st inning and another run in the top of the 2nd to make it a 6-1 game. Joe came in relief and slowed things down for a bit and Carnegie hit a solo homer to help close the gap. But Dormont didn't back down and won 9-4.

Back in an Elks uniform the Akron General Tires came to Beaver Falls for some O&P League action on the 11th. Red Whitmore was pitching and Joe was playing leftfield. Akron jumped out to a 3 run lead in the 2nd inning and never looked back. In an unfortunate play that cost the Elks a run Akron's middle fielder Hostetter hit a long fly ball out to Joe in leftfield. Joe chased the fly ball over to the foul line and dropped it. Thinking it was a foul ball he didn't pursue it, but the umpire called it a fair ball! In the meantime Hostetter was rounding the bases and scored an unusual homerun and Akron won 8-3.

As the Homestead Grays closed in on a record breaking 100 win season they met the Elks in Sharon, Pennsylvania for a double header on Sunday the 12th. The Grays play just about every day and they will play anybody willing to take them on. Baseball is a full-time job to them and as good as they are they draw in big crowds, which means money. In the morning game the Elks started Johnny Pearson and the Grays started Sam Streeter. The Grays won 3-0. In the afternoon game the

Elks started Joe and the Grays started Oscar Owens. Owens was relieved after the Elks hit him hard and Lefty Williams came in relief. But he couldn't control the hot Elks bats and the Elks won 8-1. This tied Joe's personal series with the Grays at 2-2 on the year.

Joe's brother Bill would travel around and watch Joes games and occasionally bet on them. Joe said that he won $200 betting on Joe in this game.[47]

Beaver County had a home town matchup on the 15th when the Beaver Falls Elks played the Beaver Grays, which is no relation to the Homestead Grays. Red Whitmore got the start for the Elks and Hoffmeister for the Grays. The Elks took the lead by scoring a run in the top of the 1st inning to make it 1-0. They picked up 6 more in the top of the 5th inning to make it 7-0. The Grays then yanked Hoffmeister and replaced him with Howard. In the bottom of the 5th the Gays scored 5 runs to close the gap to 7-5. The Elks relieved Whitmore and Joe came in. He slowed things down and the game went scoreless to the end and the Elks won 7-5.

With Homewood in 1st place in the Alleghany County League, with a record of 8-2, they hosted the Jimmy Smiths in a Thursday evening game on the 16th. Joe put on his Homewood uniform and took the mound against George McFarland of the Jimmy Smiths. It was a 7 inning pitching duel that was decided in the first 2 innings. Homewood score 2 runs in the 1st inning and the Jimmy Smiths scored 1 run in the 2nd inning. From there it was scoreless. Joe held the visitors to 4 hits and had just as many strikeouts. This game was crucial to Homewood maintaining 1st place and possibly winning the league title.

The picture below is as follows: Kneeling left to right: Imhoff, Hughes, F. Anthony, Captain Boll, L. Anthony, and Geisler. Standing left to right: Carnegie, Kimmick, Steele, Schultheis, Durkin, Seigfried, and manager Hank Daly. Left insert: Mullan Right insert: Joe Semler

HOMEWOOD-BRUSHTON 1928 COUNTY LOOP CHAMPIONS

Homewood-Brushton 1928[24]

Canton came to Beaver Falls on the 18th for a Saturday double header. Red Whitmore took the morning game and it was a 1-1 tie going into the bottom of the 4th inning when Ollie "Bambino" Carnegie lifted one over the left field fence for a solo homer making it 2-1. Canton had a 3-2 lead going into the bottom of the 8th inning when the Elks scored 4 runs to put the game away at 6-3. In the afternoon game Joe started against their pitcher named Leisure in a close game. Canton scored a run in the top of the 1st inning and the Elks went ahead with 2 runs in the bottom of the 2nd inning to make it 2-1. The Elks picked up another run in the bottom of the 5th inning to make it 3-1. Canton tried to rally in the top of the 9th inning but Joe held them to only 1 run and the Elks won 3-2 and swept Canton.

Joe made his minor league debut when he got a call from the Charleroi Governors saying they needed a pitcher. The Governors were in the Middle Atlantic League and classified at the Class-C level in the minors. They were getting ready to get into a series with the Scottsdale Scotties and had just released one of their pitchers, Carl Greisser. Joe agreed and made his debut with them on the 27th of August when they played their opener against Scottsdale. Joe was going up against a pitcher named Perkins. Scottsdale took the lead in the 1st inning and never relinquished it. Perkins outpitched Joe with 6 strikeouts to Joe's 3 and Perkins gave up 7 hits to Joe's 10. The Governors lost 4-2 and this was the only game Joe played with Charleroi.

Joe's connection with Charleroi was more than likely that of Joe "Lefty" Drugmond their star pitcher. Joe played a lot of games with Drugmond and I'm sure when they needed a pitcher he recommend Joe Semler. The Governors went on to place 3rd in the Mid-Atlantic League and Joe Drugmond was selected as the league's most valuable player. He received 60 votes, beating out 2nd place by 16 votes, and he received $100 (about $1,500 in 2020 money).

Even with the loss there was some good news, the Homewood Brushton team took 1st place and were declared the champions in the Alleghany County League. Although Joe only pitched 1 game for them against the Jimmy Smiths it was a crucial win.

In an unusual double header on the 1st of September the Homestead Grays played two different teams. They had won their 100th game of the season a week ago and were still looking for victims. In the first game they played the Massillon Agathons and lost to them 5-4. In their afternoon game Joe got the opportunity to play a tie breaker game against them. He had a personal 2-2 record against them this year and this was a good time to settle the issue. Pitching for the Alleghany County Champion Homewood-Brushton club Joe got the start against Sam Streeter. The game turned into a pitching battle and was called after 9 innings at a 1-1 tie. Neither pitcher gave up a home run but Streeter gave up a triple to Ollie Carnegie. Sam pitched a better game with 8 strikeouts and allowed 4 hits to Joes 5 strikeouts and 5 hits. But either way it was great pitching by both.

The Elks meet the Grays in another double header on the 13th in Sharon, Pennsylvania. The Elks lost the first game 13-2. In the nightcap Joe went up against Sam Streeter again. The "Bambino" Carnegie tripled in the 2nd inning driving in two runs and in the 7th inning Hoot Gibson drove in Johnny Pearson for the 3-2 win. So Joe was now personally 3-2 against the Homestead Grays this year.

And that was the last game of the season for the Elks. They didn't make the O&P League playoffs which were played between the Massillon Agathons and Akron General Tires. They were supposed to play the Jimmy Smiths at Born Field in Greenfield but Ed Harvey stated that the team had already disbanded for the year. Hank Daly the manager of Homewood had to do the same for a previously scheduled game because he said 7 of his starters had playoff obligations with other teams. And the Homestead Grays cancelled a double header with Homewood because they were playing out east and couldn't get back in time for the game.

It was a wild late season game played between the Homestead Grays and the Homestead All-Stars at West Field in Homewood on the 2nd of October. The All-Stars were a team put together by George Busch and made up the area's best minor league and semi-pro players. "Smokey" Joe Williams started for the Grays and Joe Semler for the All-Stars. The game was a free hitting affair and the Grays won 11-7. Williams gave up a homer and fanned 7 and Joe gave up 2 homers and fanned 1. So, Joe's personal record against the Grays went to 3-3. Just a note - "Smokey" Joe Williams is one of twelve members of the Homestead Grays Hall of Fame.

And three days later the Joe Semler verse Homestead Grays matter for this year was settled when Joe and the Homestead All-Stars played the Homestead Grays in Homestead for the final game of Joe's season. Joe was facing off against Sam Streeter and the All-Stars got the win 4-3. Joe kept the Grays to 6 hits and had 2 strikeouts. So, he ended the season 4-3 against the Grays.

That ended the season for Joe. Al finished up a pretty good season with the Stowe Civics. They didn't make any playoffs but finished 3rd in the Alleghany City League and played several post season games but didn't win any notable games.

Homewood-Brushton

1929 to 1930

Joe was back full time with the Dalymen of the Homewood-Brushton club and he picked up the nickname "Josey" in the papers. I don't know where it came from but the newspapers just started referring to him as Josey Semler. Homewood were last year's champions of the Alleghany County League but would now compete in the Inter-County League with the Beaver Falls Studebakers (yes, Ed Harvey changed the Beaver Falls team from the Elks to the Studebakers), Jimmy Smiths, Dormont, Canonsburg Gunners, Butler Armcos, Natrona, and Betlzhoover.

As for players Homewood-Brushton would field Joe Semler, Bimmy Steele and Ed Stauffeur as pitchers, Gene Gahles catcher, Dick Goldberg 1st base, Frankie "Wago" Anthony 2nd Base, Elmer Kestner shortstop, Heinie Boll 3rd base, Johnny

Pearson left field, Ollie "Bambino" Carnegie middle field, and Vern Lefty Hughes right field.

Al "Curly" Semler was playing for the Stowe Civics again in the Alleghany City League. He was also going to get a tryout with the Ed Harvey's' Studebakers to fill a vacancy in the outfield left by Hoot Gibson.

Opening day was planned for the 16th of May in Homewood-Brushton with a parade and the mayor throwing out the first pitch, but the festivities were rained out. So their first game was on the 18th at Natrona. Joe opened the season against Pickles Frederick. Homewood scored first with a run in the 2nd inning. Natrona went ahead with 2 runs in the bottom of the 6th inning to make it 2-1. Homewood tied it up in the top of the 7th inning and got the win in the 8th with 2 more runs to make it 4-3. Joe fanned 7 and hit a double.

Bad weather had again slowed the opening of a lot of games and caused plenty of cancelations. It was reported that the season may as well have just started in June for the lack of games able to be played in May.

It was finally opening day for the Homewood-Brushton club on the 1st of June against Canonsburg. In front of several thousand fans Joe faced Jewey Coen in a lopsided battle. Canonsburg took the lead 1-0 in the top of the 2nd inning and never looked back. Coen only allowed 6 hits and fanned the "Bambino" Carnegie 3 times. It was a 10-0 shutout and a game Joe and Homewood would be more than happy to forget.

Joe made up for that loss against Canonsburg when he took on the Jimmy Smiths on the 5th of June at Magee Field in Greenfield. In a must win game to hold first place Joe got the call to start. He pitched an excellent 8-2 game for the win. This placed Homewood in 1st place in the league.

Getting the start again on the 12th against last place Natrona the game was only scheduled for 5 innings. Homewood jumped out to a 7-0 lead after 2 innings. Natrona came back to score 4 more and Homewood another run for an 8-4 Homewood victory. Joe had 2 strikeouts, 2 hits, and moved Homewood to 7-1.

The picture on the following page accompanied a nice article on how tough Joe Semler and Steve Swetonic were against the Homestead Grays and how the Grays hated to face them. It stated that every club wanted a pitcher that could beat the Grays and there were few of them around. Joe was starting to be referred to as the "Poseymen Tamer." This was in reference to the longtime manager and player for the Grays named Cumberland "Cum" Posey. It went on to state that since Steve had signed with the Pittsburgh Pirates in 1929 that the job of controlling the Grays was left solely up to Joe, which he has handled well over the years. Steve would pitch for the Pirates from 1929 to 1935.

Joe Semler & Steve Swetonic[25]

Joe pitched a *"masterful[26]"* game against his longtime rivals the Homestead Grays on a Monday evening the 17th of June. Going up against Eddie Miller, Joe held the Grays to 1 run on 7 hits. He fanned 5, had 2 hits, and drove in a run in an 8-1 win. The win ended the Grays 14 game win streak.

He played the Grays again on the 25th but this time he was suited up as a Youngstown Oakland, which was basically the Homewood club wearing Oakland uniforms. Playing at Idora Park in Youngstown a guy by the name of Teddy Bair started for Oakland and Elbert Williams for the Grays. Down 5-1 in the 5th inning Joe came in relief of Bair and held the Grays hitless for the remainder of the game. The Oakland's picked up another run in the bottom of the 9th inning to make it a 5-2 win for the Grays.

Although Ted Bair was the pitchers real name, Joe said that guys would pitch under an alias so they wouldn't be recognized. He said that he had even pitched under the name "Irwin" in Parkersburg, West Virginia and Waynesburg, Pennsylvania.[47] I think the reason they would play under an alias was because they were under contract to play for a certain team and didn't want to break that deal. So they would go pitch under an alias. Joe said when he would do it he would get $50 a game plus expenses.[47] He said the way it worked was a team would call up Honus Wagner and say they needed a pitcher for a certain game. Honus would call a pitcher like Joe up and ask him if he wanted the job. If he took it he got $50 and Honus got a fee for sending him.

Joe said he was headed down to Waynesburg one time to do a job for Honus and he saw Leo Carroll on the same train. He went and sat next to him and asked him where he was going. It turned out they were headed to the same game and both were sent by Honus. Joe asked him who he was going to pitch for and he said Saxonville Stogies, (although I think he meant the Wheeling Stogies) did you ever hear of them? Joe said no, but that's who I'm supposed to pitch for. They agreed that they would figure it out when they got there. When they arrived at the game the team's manager said Joe was supposed to pitch the first 5 innings and Leo the remainder of the game. Joe pitched his required 5 innings without giving up a hit. He said he wanted to stay in the game since he was doing so well, and won the game allowing only one hit.[47]

Joe and the Homewood club traveled to Canonsburg on the 29th of June. It was a battle between 1st place Homewood and 2nd place Canonsburg. Joe was facing Earl Mosely who you will remember was an ex-major leaguer. The Gunners got ahead early to a 2-0 lead and held it until the top of the 4th inning when Homewood tied it at 2-2. They tagged on 2 more in the 7th inning and 4 more in the 9th inning for an 8-2 win. Joe held the Gunners to 6 hits and fanned 3. The win put Homewood at 12-1 and Canonsburg at 8-4. The only league loss so far this year for Homewood was when they beat Joe in the season opener.

As the teams in the Inter-County league went into July it marked the beginning of the 2nd half of the leagues season. Game cancellations caused by bad weather along with poor attendance caused the Beaver Falls Studebakers and Natrona to drop out of the league. The league decided to carry on with just six teams and the voids in the schedule caused by the teams that dropped out could be filled by playing out of league opponents.

The J.L. Thomas club from the Alleghany City League came to Homewood on Friday the 5th of July. Johnny Pearson got the start and surprisingly the city club got ahead 5-2 after 3 innings. Joe, who was playing right field, came in relief and slowed them down but the Homewood bats were cold and they lost 7-3.

Homewood met up with the Homestead Grays for a 6:15pm game at Homewood Field on the 10th. And of course Homewood started Joe who went up against "Smokey" Joe Williams. The Grays were up 6-3 going into the bottom of the 7th inning. Joe was on 3rd base when the batter hit a light tap to the pitcher and Joe tried to make it home. As he slid into home plate he collided with Buck Ewing, the catcher, and was knocked unconscious! He was so banged up that he couldn't continue the game and Ed Stauffeur came in relief. The Grays ended up winning the game 6-4. Before Joe was injured he had fanned 6 and hit a double.

The Inter-county league closed out its first half and Homewood-Brushton was crowned the winner. Going into the 2nd half all the teams had to cut their rosters to 18 men and could not sign any new players. This was to prevent teams from stacking their roster going into the second half.

Homewood had been without their star 3rd baseman Heinie Boll for a few weeks due to an injured shoulder and was hoping to get him back for the 2nd half. Joe was said to be recovering well after being knocked out in the game with the Grays.

Joe got his first start since being knocked unconscious against Canonsburg on the 26th at home. Facing Jewey Coen, Joe had his hands full. The Gunners ace had one of the best days of his career fanning 9 and in 6 of 9 innings retiring Homewood in order. But Joe wasn't doing too bad himself and had 4 strikeouts and his team's defense was in top form. Befitting the great game on both sides it ended in a 3-3 tie.

With a team mostly made up of Homewood players Frank Mills once again formed the Youngstown Oakland's to face the Pittsburgh Pirates in an exhibition game in Youngstown, Ohio on the 28th of July. The game was played at Idora Park in front of 4,000 fans and drew in $3,500 at the box office. Joe only pitched an inning and Bimmy Steele and Leo Carroll pitched 4 innings each. The Pirates had been experiencing a lot of injuries lately and didn't want what was left of their stars, like Lloyd Waner and Adam Comorosky, hurt in this exhibition game and yanked them after the 1st inning. The Pirates still won 9-5 in a 9 inning game.

To close out July Joe got the start against the Jimmy Smiths on the 31st. Playing at Born Field in Greenfield Joe went all 9 innings. Jumping out to a 3-0 lead in the top of the 1st inning Homewood never looked back in a 5-3 win.

As the teams entered August they dropped down to 5 teams as the Butler Armcos dropped out because of low fan turn out and depleted finances. And the Beltzhoovers were barely hanging on. They were losing their home field at Mckinley Park due to a road being built through it. And to make matters worse they were in the red financially and had poor fan support.

To try and drum up money teams were doing anything to draw a crowd. Even Hank Daly squeezed everything he could get out of the Homewood club. His latest money making venture was playing the Chicago Ranger Girls, a traveling all women's baseball team. And to add to the novelty he put a local 16 year old girl from Homewood on the mound, named Dolly Finn, to pitch against the Ranger Girls. Playing to a record crowd in Homewood she was backed up by Homewood's regular line up including Joe in right field. Dolly did a fantastic job! She pitched all 9 innings, struck out 2, and won 14-10. Joe helped out with 2 hits.

Playing on the Oakland team again Joe pitched against the Homestead Grays at Idora Park in front of another large crowd on the 4th of August. Joe was pitching against Sam Streeter. Oakland was ahead 5-3 after 5 innings and the Grays relieved Streeter and brought in "Smokey" Joe Williams. He got rocked for 3 runs in the bottom of the 6th inning bringing Oakland's lead to 8-3. Then in the top of the 7th inning the Grays picked up 3 runs to make it 8-6. And in the top of the 8th inning Joe Semler got rocked for 3 more runs and fell behind 9-8. That was it for Joe and he was relieved by Bimmy Steele. Oakland scored a run in the bottom of the 8th inning to tie the game at 9-9. It went scoreless in the 9th inning and went into extra innings. The Grays picked up a run in the top of the 10th inning and Oakland was silent in the bottom of the inning giving the Grays a 10-9 win.

Still wearing a Youngstown Oakland's jersey on the 8th, Joe was slated to get the start against the Brooklyn Dodgers at Idora Park with Bimmy Steele again in reserve. But instead, the exhibition game had Humphrey's starting for the Oakland's and Clise Dudley for the Dodgers.

Joe's former teammate Billy Rhiel was now playing for the Dodgers and he was from Youngstown. In honor of his return home Youngstown declared the day "Billy Rhiel Day" and he was presented with a check for $500 from the Billy Rhiel Booster Club in front of 2,000 hometown fans. The pre-game festivities also included the famous World Boxing Champion James J. Corbett throwing out the ceremonial first pitch of the game.

The Dodgers came out strong with their regular starting lineup and were ahead 6-1 at the end of the 3rd inning. Joe came in relief and settled the Dodgers down. The Oakland's started to rally and Dudley was relieved by Luther Roy in the 6th inning. By this time the Dodgers were only ahead 6-4. The Oakland's scored another run in the 7th inning and in the 8th inning they scored 4 runs on 4 hits to take a 9-6 lead - Elmer Kestner walked, Joe Semler grounded out, Frank Fitch singled, and Frey singled scoring Kestner. Then Heinie Boll hit a long double scoring Fitch and Frey. Vern Hughes walked, Ollie

Carnegie struck out and Rhiney Kress singled scoring Boll. Rittenhouse finally flied out to end the inning.

In the 9th inning Joe finally gave up a run when Brooklyn's 1st baseman Del Bissonette hit a solo homer off of him. It was said to be one of the longest drives ever hit at Idora Park and it cleared the roller coaster in center field. But that was all the Dodgers could get off of Joe and he held on to win the game 9-7.

After the amazing come from behind win the crowd went crazy. And Joe said he vividly remembers James J. Corbett coming out onto the field and shaking his hand and saying to him *"boy did you give me a big thrill watching you beat those Dodgers. You really pitched a good ball game son."*[47] You can hear it in his voice as he retold that story to my dad on the audio cassette, that game was a very fond memory to Joe.

Joe got another chance at the Homestead Grays at home on the Homewood Playground Field. It was a Saturday night crowd pleaser on the 10th of August and Joe was matched up against Eddie Miller. Joe looked like he was in big trouble in the top of the 1st inning when the Grays scored 5 runs. But Homewood answered with 3 runs in the bottom of the inning to make it a 5-3 game. And in the bottom of the 2nd inning they scored 2 more runs to tie it at 5-5. The Grays jumped back ahead in the top of the 3rd with 2 runs to make it 7-5. Joe held them scoreless for the remainder of the game while Homewood picked up 2 runs in the bottom of the 5th inning to tie it 7-7. And then in the bottom of the 6th inning Elmer Kestner singled driving in Johnny Pearson for the 8-7 winning run. Joe had a double driving in 2 runs.

It was a highly touted game for 1st place in the Inter-County standings as Homewood hosted Canonsburg on the 14th. Calling on their star pitcher Homewood sent Joe to the mound and the Gunners sent their ace Jewey Coen. Homewood jumped out to a 3-0 lead at the bottom of the 1st inning and never gave it up. Four errors by Canonsburg and great defense like a throw from Heine Boll to get a Gunner out at the plate highlighted the 5-3 win. Joe's record against the ex-major leaguer Jewey Coen was 1 win, 1 loss, and a tie so far this year.

Putting on an Oakland uniform Joe was once again lined up against the Homestead Grays and their pitcher George Britt. Joe was personally 2-2 against the Grays so far this year. It didn't start out well for Joe and after giving up 5 runs after 2 innings he was relieved by Humphrey. He settled the Grays down and only allowed 2 more runs. But Oakland's bats were cold and Britt pitched a fine game for a 7-2 win.

Traveling on the 28th of August to Canonsburg, in a critical game in the 2nd half of the Inter-County League Championship, Homewood once again put their ace Joe Semler up against the Gunner ace Jewey Coen. In front of a packed crowd at Beck Field visiting Homewood jumped out to a 5-1 lead by the 3rd inning. The Gunners relieved Coen and brought in another ex-major leaguer Earl Mosely. He was immediately rocked for 5 runs in the top of the 4th inning making it a 10-1 game. The Gunners started to whittle away at Joe but he held them off and

Homewood won 14-8. Joe fanned 6 and had 2 hits, with one being a double.

As the Press-Beaver County League started to get ready for their playoffs the Elwood City team signed several Homewood players, including Joe, to play for them. On the 29th of August Joe got the call to start in the second game of the playoffs when Ellwood City was hosting the Rochester Whippets. Joe was going up against their ace Hoffman. Ellwood City scored first in the bottom of the 2nd inning and Rochester tied it up in the top of the 4th inning at 2-2. Ellwood City went ahead 3-2 in the bottom of the 4th inning and Rochester tied it up again in the top of the 7th inning at 3-3. The game was called after 7 innings of play due to darkness.

As for the Homewood-Brushton team, they won the Inter-County Championship by winning the 1st and 2nd half of the season. Pictured below are back row left to right: Joe Kline, Ollie Carnegie, Joe Semler, Bill Sholtheis, Ray Burke, Elmer Kestner, Scott Morgan, Heinie Boll (captain), Dick Goldberg, Vern Hughes, and Councilman John Herron. Front row left to right: Manager Hank Daly, Johnny Pearson, Gene Gahles, Frank Anthony, Ed Stauffer, Bimmy Steel, and Larry Anthony.

Homewood-Brushston 1929[27]

In the fourth game of the Rochester verse Ellwood City series Joe got the start. The score was 13-3 going into the top of the 9th inning and Joe was just cruising along pitching a nice game and with plenty of offensive support. But he almost let it slip away in the top of the 9th when Rochester scored 6 runs to bring the game to 13-9. But that was all they could score and Joe held on to the win. The series standing was Rochester 2, Ellwood City 1, and 1 tie. In order to win the series a team had to win 3 games. After this 4th game an argument broke out between the two teams as to where the next game was to be played and if they would even play another game.

Homewood and the Homestead Grays got into a three game series to decide who the Pittsburgh Area Independent Champions would be in mid-September. In the first game Homewood started Ed Stouffer against "Smokey" Joe Williams and the Grays won 4-1. The second game was played a few days later and all indications were that Hank Daly would start Joe Semler, but instead started Ed Stouffer again against "Smokey" Joe Williams. The game was only to be 7 innings and was held at Homewood. It was scoreless going into the top of the 4th inning when the Grays scored a run to make it 1-0. Homewood answered in the bottom of the 5th inning with 4 runs to make it 4-1. The 6th inning was scoreless and in the top of the 7th inning the Grays started to rally. After scoring 2 runs Joe came in relief to hold the 4-3 win. They didn't get the 3rd game in to decide the winner so the championship series ended in a tie.

The Homestead Grays faced off against the Homestead All-stars at West Field in Homestead on the 24th of September. Joe got the start against "Smokey" Joe Williams in what turned into a 20-1 blowout in favor of the Grays. Even after Joe gave up 11 runs in the top of the 3rd inning he stayed in for the full 6 inning game and continued on with the beating. It's not like Joe didn't have any backup, minor leaguers Leo Mackey was there along with Homewood team mates Ollie the "Bambino" Carnegie, Elmer Kestner, and Johnny Pearson. But you had to bring your "A" game every time you faced the Grays or they would beat you bad. So, Joe ended his personal record with the Grays this year at 2-3.

It was Semler verse Semler once again as Al "Curly" Semler and the Stowe Civics took on Joe Semler and the Powell Minor League All-Stars. They met up in a Sunday night game at Reliance Field in McKees Rocks. The game came down to the 9th inning when the All-Stars took a 3-2 lead. In the bottom of the 9th Curly came up to bat and took his brother for a 2 run walk off homer winning the game for the Stowe Civics! Curly had 3 hits driving in 2 runs and Joe fanned 7.

And the 1929 season couldn't have ended any better than a game between two brothers in their home town of McKees Rocks.

1930:

The 1930's were the start of the Great Depression in America. But for the most part baseball seemed unaffected going into April as team managers started to gather their teams and sign players. Just as leagues had come and gone in previous years, this year was no different. The Inter-County league was gone and teams like Homewood-Brushton and the Jimmy Smiths had discussed merging. They figured they might have a better chance with a combined team out in the independent circuit, but the venture fell through. The Jimmy Smiths and Homewood-Brushton ended up in the West-Penn league. They played league teams and anyone else they could to make money. Joe signed with Homewood again and was reported to be also pitching some games with Stowe and possibly even a third club.

The Homewood-Brushton team would be made up with Red Bierwirth catching, Joe Semler, Bimmy Steele, and Buck Jones as pitchers, Dave Wickline 1st base, Frank Anthony 2nd base, Elmer Kestner short stop, Heinie Boll 3rd base, Hoot Gibson left field, Toby Uansa middle field and Johnny Pearson right field. They also had Ollie Carnegie as another outfielder and Larry Anthony as an infielder

Al Semler was sticking with Stowe again in the Alleghany City League

Joe started off the year with a bang pitching the areas first no-hit and no run game against the Universal club who played in the West-Penn league. He was one strikeout away from a perfect game, the best a pitcher can perform.

Traveling to Verona on the 8th of May Joe got the start with Homewood against Verona's' Buzz Isherwood. Both pitched a nice game with Joe fanning 8 and giving up 6 hits and Isherwood fanning 5 and giving up 4 hits. After 9 innings it ended in a 1-1 tie.

On the 24th of May the Homestead Grays racked up their 30th victory this season against Joe and Homewood at Forbes Field. The picture on the previous page accompanied the box score. Playing in a 6:30pm game Joe got behind early and was down 6-0 after 6 innings. Then in the 7th inning the Grays got 5 runs off of him making it 11-0. That was enough to bring Bimmy Steele in relief and the score stood 11-0 after 9 innings for a Gray's win.

Joe Semler 1930[28]

It wasn't getting any better for Joe when he and Homewood traveled to Dormont on the 27th for a 7 inning game. Joe was facing Leo Carroll. His Dormont team jumped out to a 5 run lead in the bottom of the 1st inning and they didn't look back cruising to a 6-2 win. This was Homewood's first West-Penn League loss of the season making them 4-1.

It took Al and the Stowe Civics to finally end the Homestead Grays win streak at 33 games on the 28th. Although the Grays pitcher Darltie Cooper held Stowe to only 2 hits they capitalized on them for a 2-0 win. Al played middle field and was hitless.

Joe and a majority of the Homewood team also played for a team called the Fosterville Merchants, who were basically the Oakland's from last year. On the 1st of June they took on the Akron Goodyear's in Youngstown, Ohio. Joe was going up against a lefty known as Joe Horan. Goodyear got the 1st run in the top of the 2nd inning. But the Merchants came back to tie it in the bottom of the 4th inning when Elmer Kestner walked, then Dick Goldberg flied to centerfield but the centerfielder dropped the ball. Retrieving the ball he threw it wildly towards 3rd base and Kestner scored. Then in the 6th inning the Merchants scored 2 more runs when Frank Fitch singled to left, Kestner advanced him with a bunt, but was put out at 1st base. Goldberg once again flied to center and once again the center fielder dropped the ball! Making another wild throw towards 3rd base Fitch scored. Ollie Carnegie then singled and drove in Goldberg for the 3-1 win.

Joe finally gets a win for Homewood on the 2nd of June when Homewood played the Whitaker club on the road. Homewood jumped out to a 3-0 lead in the top of the 1st inning giving Joe breathing room to fan 6 and hold on to a 5-4 win after 9 innings.

After nearly pitching a perfect game against the Universal club earlier in the year Joe got the call against them again on the 5th. Playing at Universal Joe had another great outing allowing only 4 hits and fanning 6 in a 5-0 win.

Al Semler and the Stowe Civics played a game at Homewood on Saturday the 7th of June. Curly was playing middle Field and Bimmy Steele was pitching for Homewood. It was a back and forth game that ended in a 7-7 tie after 8 innings.

June was proving to be a good month for Joe and it got even better on the 13th in a Friday evening game against N. Bessemer at home. Holding the visitors to 6 hits Joe got 2 hits himself and drove in a run in a massive 13-1 win.

Getting a crack at another "tire" team Joe and the Fosterville Merchants took on the Firestone Nonskids in Youngstown on Sunday the 15th. Joe was matched up against Bozo Miller in a nice pitching duel for the first 3 innings. But the Firestones started to gain some runs and by the end of the 6th inning it was 5-1. In the top of the 7th inning the Merchants started to gain some traction when Joe singled to drive in a run and so did Fitch to make it a 5-3 game. But that is all the Merchants could do and the game ended with the Firestones winning 5-3. Joe did manage to hold the Firestones best hitter ever, Ray

Burris, hitless in the game and they said it was their toughest matchup so far this year. Joe ended up with 3 strikeouts, a hit, and drove in a run.

Getting back into a winning groove Joe and Homewood took on the Wilmerding Airbrake club on the 19th. Joe was on his game striking out 10 and leading Homewood to a 1-0 win. Homewood hardened their 1st place position in the West-Penn League at 10-1.

The Semler brothers met again when Joe and Homewood traveled to play Stowe on the 27th of June for a Saturday evening game. Joe put on a pitching clinic fanning 10 and giving up only 8 hits in a 4-1 game. Stowe got their 1 run in the 1st inning and that was it for the remaining 8 innings. Al did manage to get 2 of those hits off of Joe, one being a double.

The Dormont club, which is probably the biggest threat to Homewood in the West-Penn League, came to Homewood for a July 4th double header. The afternoon game was a 16-15 barn burner won by Homewood with Johnny Pearson getting the win. The evening game was between Joe and Dormont's Chuck Dunn. It was another close one and Dormont won it 6-5 with a 9th inning 2 run rally.

But for some reason Homewood-Brushton and Dormont, who were in 1st and 2nd place respectively in the West-Penn League, decided to leave the league and enter the Alleghany City League. There had been some speculation towards the end of June that Dormont might switch leagues. And Homewood said if Dormont left so would they. Because not only was Dormont their only competition in the league but they had a huge fan base that drew in a lot of money.

In their first City League game Joe got the start against the J.L. Thomas club on the 7th of July. Joe was in rare form defensively throwing 7 strikeouts in an 11-3 win. Offensively he had a single, double and a homerun. Johnny Pearson also had a homer. After the game Joe was heard telling his teammates *"Don't we pitchers hit them!"*[29]

Frank Mills put together another team made up mostly of Homewood players called the Coshocton's to take on the Pittsburgh Pirates in an exhibition game. They played at Lake Park in Coshocton, Ohio on the 10th of July.

In the pre-game warmups Adam Comorosky, the Pirates outfielder, came up and started to talk to Joe and Toby Uansa. Comorosky asked Joe how much he was making in the semi-pros. Joe said he was making $250 a month as a carpenter, $135 from Homewood, and $50 a game plus expenses pitching games like this exhibition game. He figured it ended up being about $600-$700 a month.[47]

Joe got the start against Marty Lang. Now the Pirates were not phoning this game in and had their starting lineup facing Joe - guys like Paul Waner, Gus Suhr, and Pie Traynor. And they just beat Joe up for 6 runs by the 7th inning. Jenkins, a local pitcher, came in relief and they took him for 10 runs to include a grand slam homer. The Coshocton's finally scored 3 runs in the 9th inning to at least escape a shutout. The final score was 16-3.

It wasn't as if the Coshocton's were expected to beat the Pirates, they were two steps down from the major leagues, but they weren't expected to get their clock cleaned. All the papers said it was embarrassing. And I think the reason Coshocton took so much heat from the sports writers was that they played sloppily, committing 6 errors and basically giving the Pirates 12 of their 16 runs.

Coming off the disaster in Coshocton Joe was back in a Homewood uniform the next day pitching against the North Side Civics in the City League, a team which included Art and Jim Rooney. It was a much better outing for Joe as he held the Civics to 7 hits and threw 4 strikeouts in a 10-2 win.

In their first meeting with Dormont since they both joined the City League Joe started against Leo Carroll in a highly publicized game. Hoot Gibson was injured in the 3rd inning when he tripped over a sewer pipe that was exposed out in left field. Lefty Hughes came in to replace him. Dormont was leading 8-3 going into the 5th inning when Joe started to lose control and Carl Stewart came in relief. He was a bit wild to start with but held Dormont to only 1 more run in the game. Stewart had to also be relieved in the 5th inning by Chuck Dunn and he allowed 4 runs, but kept the lead and 9-7 win.

Playing on the road in a Friday night game on the 18th Homewood took on the J.L. Thomas squad. Carl Stewart got the start for Homewood but after giving up 10 runs in the bottom of the 3rd inning Joe came in relief. Behind 12-2 Joe tried to cool the Thomas bats but they were only playing a 7 inning game so there wasn't much room to gain ground. Thomas won it 16-10. Homewood were tied in 4th place with the Stowe Civics and Dormont. J.L Thomas was in 3rd place.

I had mentioned earlier that the first major league night game wouldn't be played until 1935, but the first time it was tried at Forbes field was on the 19th of July 1930. The Negro League's Homestead Grays played the Kansas City Monarchs in a game that started at 9:15pm. Over 6,000 fans packed Forbes Field to witness the sight of 33 flood lights being powered by huge generators lighting up the field of play. The game was deemed a success in some ways but there was the noise of the generators and the newness of playing under artificial light.

Joe should have had an easy game against the last place Pleasant Valley Smilers on the 22nd, but the Homewood bats were quiet. None the less Joe only allowed 7 hits and threw 4 strikeouts and edged Pleasant Valley 2-1 for a win.

Tied with the J.L Thomas club for 1st place in the City League Homewood faced 3rd place Book Shoe on the 25th at home. Book Shoe had won the 1st half of the City League Pennant and was a tough team. Joe got the start and Homewood jumped out to a 1-0 lead in the 1st inning. Then Book Shoe scored 2 runs in the 2nd inning and 4 runs in the 4th inning to make it a 6-1 game. Joe pitched pretty well and held the Book Shoe club to less hits than Homewood and fanned 8, but it just wasn't enough and Book Shoe won 6-3. The loss dropped Homewood to 3rd place and propelled Book Shoe in a tie for 1st place with J.L. Thomas.

Getting another shot at Book Shoe on the 5th of August Joe got the start at home. His team gave him a nice 8-0 lead after 2 innings and Joe cruised to a 9-4 win. He helped himself with a double which drove in a run and threw 4 strikeouts. The win placed Homewood in 1st place with a comfortable 4 game lead on the J.L. Thomas club.

Nursing an injured back "Smoky" Joe Semler took the mound on the 20th against the Pleasant Valley Smilers. Homewood had the bats working and got Joe out to a nice 5-0 lead which he kept until the last inning when he gave up a run to make the final 5-1. He pitched a nice game only giving up 6 hits and he hit a double. If you noticed I referred to Joe as "Smoky." This is the first time I have seen him referred to as "Smoky" Joe Semler in the papers. I'm assuming he picked up the nick name due to his fast ball.

With the City Leagues 2nd half Pennant on the line Joe took the mound on the 25th against Pleasant Valley again. "Smoky" Joes back wasn't bothering him today and he put on a fantastic performance. Homewood scored 6 runs in the 2nd inning and 4 more in the 4th inning to give him a 10-0 shutout win. Joe did his part keeping the Smilers to only 3 hits and striking out 2.

The City League championship would be between Book Shoe and Homewood. Book Shoe won the 1st half of the season's pennant and came in 3rd in the 2nd half with a record of 11-10. Homewood joined the league at the end of the 1st half and won the 2nd half with a record of 16-5.

The first game of the 5 game series was played on Thursday the 28th at Olympia Park on Mt. Washington. Nearly 3,000 fans turned out to see Book Shoe win with a score of 8-6. The Shoemen started Gus Otey against Homewood's Bimmy Steele. Steele got behind 7-2 by the 3rd inning and was relieved by Carl Stewart. Homewood started to come back towards the end but a sensational catch by Book Shoe's outfielder with 2 men on and 2 outs saved the game for them.

The second scheduled game on Friday the 29th was sort of controversial in that it was called off due to rain that had moved through Homewood's Playground Field around 4pm. The visiting team, along with fans and sports writers, upon arriving for the 6pm game thought the field was fine and wanted to play. But Homewood said the field wasn't playable and cancelled the game. The Shoemen thought that Homewood was trying to get out of the game for some reason and said if Homewood didn't want to play the next game that they would take the title! The teams agreed that the game would be rescheduled for Tuesday at Olympia Park.

The next game that was scheduled to be at Olympia Park was eventually played back at Playground Field on Tuesday the 2nd of September in front of a crowd of about 2,000. Homewood tied the series up with a 6-3 win. Homewood started "Lefty" Brinker and the Shoemen started their spitball ace "Buck" Jones. Homewood got out to an early 1st inning lead and held it the entire game.

The 3rd game was played Thursday the 4th back at Olympia Park. Joe got the start and took Homewood to a 1-0 win and a 2-1 lead in the series. Pitching against Steve Roscoe they both pitched a great game only allowing 6 hits and 3 strikeouts each. Roscoe gave up the winning run in the top of the 2nd inning when he walked Heinie Boll, who was advanced to 3rd off a double by Jimmy Durkin, and driven home on a single by Toby Uansa.

Game 4 was played on Friday the 5th in front of 2,800 fans at Homewood Field and they took the title of 1930 City League Champions! Carl Stewart had one of his best performances with Homewood as he mixed up his curve, spit, and fast balls, leading the team to a 10-4 win. Book Shoe had gone up first scoring 2 runs in the top of the 1st inning but Homewood came up with 9 runs in the bottom of the 2nd inning to put it away. The Shoemen threw Gus Oatey, "Buck" Jones, and Chuck Dunn at Homewood without success.

And that's how the season ended for Joe. He only had the one game against the Homestead Grays in which he lost. Homewood had played them in a double header in early July and Carl Stewart got the loss in the early game and Bimmy Steele was beaten in the nightcap.

The City League published their All-Star team and Joe made the 2nd team behind Bimmy Steele on the 1st team.

Al Semler with Stowe finished in a three way tie for last place in the City League. He personally had a good year and got an honorable mention in the City League All-Star team. He would go on to play for Homewood-Brushton next year.

Hazleton Mountaineers 1931 to 1932

In March several local businessmen from the South Hills section of Pittsburgh purchased the Hazleton Mountaineers, a minor league baseball club in the New York – Pennsylvania League. Located about 250 miles from Pittsburgh it's a little town just south of Wilkes-Barre and Scranton. The new owners hired a local Pittsburgh semi-pro player named Hubert "Hubie" Fitzgerald to manage and play for the team. He in turn scouted the local Pittsburgh area for players to take with him to Hazleton. Among the players he signed were Joe Semler and Elmer Kestner.

Hazleton was in the Pittsburgh Pirates farm system, which meant as you progressed you would eventually work up to them in the major leagues. They were considered to be at the class-B level in the minor league system which was entry level. Class-A would be the next step higher, then the major leagues.

The following is the 1931 team as it was published on the 31st of March in The Plain Speaker, a local Hazleton paper. Of course their line-up changed continuously as players were added and dropped through the season. But I thought it was interesting and sort of reads like a scouting report.

"*Hubert J. Fitzgerald*, manager, outfielder - Height 5 feet 6 inches; weight, 140 pounds. Bats and throws left. Age, 24. Home, Pittsburgh, Pa. First started pro ball in 1927 and played with Albany, Syracuse, Hazleton and New York. Last year's batting record; 565 Ab, 103 Runs, 171 Hits, 19 2b, 10 3b, 1 HR, 26 Sb, .303 Avr.

Gerald F. Fitzgerald, outfielder – Height, 5 feet 9 inches; weight, 155pounds. Bats and throws left. Age 23. Home, Pittsburgh, Pa. First played pro ball at Newark under Walter Johnson in 1928. Played at Newark and Albany in 1929 and at Albany all last year, 1930. Last year's batting record; 666 Ab, 108 Runs, 210 Hits, 30 2b, 13 3b, 3 HR, 18 Sb, .316 Avr.

Lamar "Mickey" Bell, outfielder – Height, 6 feet 1 inch; weight, 180 pounds. Bats and throws right. Age 21. Home, Shenandoah, Pa. Played at Hagerstown in Blue Ridge last year and on disbandment of league became free agent. Record 1930; 317 Ab, 57 Runs, 117 Hits, 20 2b, 9 3b, 17 HR, 18 Sb, .369 Avr.

George Thomas, first baseman and outfielder – Height, 5 feet 10-1/2 inches; weight. 170. Age, 28. Home Spring City, Pa. Acquired in deal with Dick Hughes for Stan Lewan. Has *lifetime batting average of .323 for eight seasons and is one of the hardest and timeliest hitters in the league.*

Thomas Clancy, *second baseman – Age 25. Home, Somerville, Mass. Height, 5 feet 10 inches; weight, 165 pounds. Acquired from Wilkes-Barre in 1930, farmed to Cumberland and recalled. Has played in Three-I League.*

Elmer Kestner, *shortstop – Age, 22; Height, 5 feet 11 inches; weight, 160 pounds. Home at Pittsburgh, Pa. Has played in best semi-pro leagues in western Pennsylvania and Ohio for last three years and last spring went south with Cleveland Indians, but was farmed to the Three-I League before season opened, refused to play there and asked for release, which was granted. Has decided to have another try at pro ball. Is a very fine fielder and fair hitter, with prospects of becoming good hitter.*

Richard Hughes, *third baseman – Age, 28; height, 5 feet 9 inches; weight, 160 pounds. Home, Holliday's Cove, W. Va. Classed as finest fielder and one of the smartest base runners in the league. At Harrisburg five years prior to joining Hazleton. Change of teams should give him his best year.*

Francis O'Haren, *third base – Age, 22; height, 5 feet 11 inches; weight, 175 pounds. Home, Shenandoah, Pa. Rookie prospect who played at Georgetown University. Big, strong and fast. May develop into a real threat for a regular job.*

Ralph Shultz, *first base and outfield – Age, 22; height, 5 feet 11 inches; weight, 175 pounds. Home at East Liverpool, O.*

Has played fast semi-pro ball in Ohio for three or four years, compiling a sensational batting and fielding record. Good prospects.

Jack Ernst, catcher – Age, 28; height; 5 feet 11 inches; weight 180 pounds. Home, Williamsport, Pa. One of the most valuable players in the league, due to his all around ability to play infield, outfield or catch. A hustler and good hitter, and if played steadily behind the plate has a fine chance to go higher, for good catchers are more and more in demand by big leagues and higher minors.

Walter Latusick, catcher – Age 23; height, 5 feet 10-1/2 inches; weight 170 pounds. Home, Pittsburgh, Pa. Rookie prospect from semi-pro circles around western Pennsylvania. Has fine chance to stay as second string catcher. Good thrower and worker and should develop into a valuable aid to Ernst.

William Lesky, catcher – Age, 21; height, 5 feet 11 inches; weight, 180 pounds. Home at Gilberton, Pa. Big, strong, young prospect who will battle Latusick for second string job. Comes highly recommended and may prove the man needed.

John Rosser, right hand pitcher – Rookie from Mahanoy City, Pa.

Mike Ferrence, right hand pitcher – Beaver Meadoe.

Emil Sagehorn, right hand pitcher – Trenton, N.J.

Art Johnson, *left hander – Warren, Pa. Holdover from last year, acquired from York. Had bad year last year, but has a lot of stuff. May be traded or sold before season starts.*

Dewey Hinkle, *left hander – Montclair, N.J. – Came to Hazleton from Reading and had a fairly good record, winning four and losing five, but beating Wilkes-Barre three times. Should have fine year with average club behind him.*

Joseph Semler, *right hander – Pittsburgh, Pa. Has been best semi-pro pitcher in Pittsburgh leagues and Eastern Ohio for three years or more. Has deceptive side arm delivery with good fast ball and fine control. Is counted on to be a regular starting pitcher.*

Eddie Mahon, *left hander – Philadelphia, Pa. Good looking rookie prospect who has pitched fine semi-pro ball around Philly.*

E.S. Novey, *right hander – Pittsburgh, Pa. A young speed ball flinger who is best prospect for sale on club, if he develops as he should."*

One other outfielder was signed but didn't want his name published in the paper. This was Ollie "Bambino" Carnegie. He had signed but didn't report to play until late July. He wasn't planning on playing in the minors but after losing his job with the railroad because of the Great Depression he had no choice.

Two other guys on the team that played in the same circuit as Joe back in Pittsburgh were Walter Latusick and Ed Novey. Latusick played for the Book Shoe club last year and Novey played for the J.L. Thomas club last year.

The team started to report for two weeks of spring training on the 14th of April at Slatington, Pa. which is about 45 minutes northwest of Hazleton. Joe was late arriving because of tryouts with the Pittsburgh Pirates. The Mountaineers manager, Hubie Fitzgerald, was also in Pittsburgh meeting with Barney Dreyfuss, the owner of the Pirates, to see about getting some Pirate rookies to come play for Hazleton. This was pretty common and all the teams tried to get the major league team they were under to send players down. This helped boost fan attendance at the games and helped them out when they were behind in the league standings.

As the Mountaineers reported to Slatington they were booked into a local hotel and began practicing and holding exhibition games at the local ballfield, Victory Park. They also made trips back to Hazleton to play exhibition games and the local papers were abuzz with excitement about the start of the season. Probably one of the more interesting teams that Hazleton played in exhibition was the Detroit Clowns. They traveled the country like the Homestead Grays, and the House of David, earning a living. They drew crowds because they were a good team, played dressed as clowns, and clowned around with the opposing team and fans.

The Mountaineers home games were played at Buhler Stadium which was located close to the center of Hazleton. In preparation for the upcoming season they had just added an additional 1,200 seats that increased their capacity to 4000 people. Because the area had not adopted to daylight savings time games were played in the late afternoon during the week to attract office workers, store employees, and miners getting off of work. They also played on Sunday afternoons. Tickets cost between .50 cents for general admission and a $1.00 for box seats.

Just before opening day on the 5th of May Joe's back was giving him problems. He had pitched an exhibition game against the House of David and strained it. To add to the Mountaineers pitching problems Ed Novey, who had been sick with the grippe, was now out with a sore arm.

Joe opened his season for Hazleton on the 10th of May when they traveled to play a double header against the Williamsport Grays. Joe's back wasn't giving him any problems as he masterfully handled the Grays holding them to only 4 hits, throwing 4 strikeouts, and getting a hit himself in a 3-1 win. It was a great way to start out in the minor leagues. Hazleton didn't fare as well in the second game and Dewey Hinkle got the 6-4 loss.

Getting his second win in as many games Joe started against the Scranton Miners in front of 600 home field fans on Thursday the 14th. Hazleton won 8-2 and Joe gave up only 2 runs, both homers, and allowed only 8 hits. Joe had 2 strikeouts and hit a double driving in a run. Besides the 2 homers he gave up the other 6 hits were just singles.

The team was on the road the 18th against last year's league pennant winning Wilkes-Barre Barons. Joe got the start looking for 3 wins in a row. Hazleton was ahead 4-3 but Joe let the Barons get ahead of him in the bottom of the 4th inning allowing 4 runs which gave the Barons a 7-4 win.

In a double header against the Barons in Wilkes-Barre on the 20th the Mountaineers dropped the first game 6-4. The second game was scheduled for 7 innings but after being tied 2-2 it went into extra innings. In the bottom of the 8th inning Joe came in relief with 2 outs and no one on base. The first batter singled along with the second batter. The third batter was intentionally walked. With the bases loaded Joe accidentally hit the fourth batter in the ribs, walking in the winning run for the Barons. It was a tough loss for Joe and the sweep by the Barons put the Mountaineers in last place in the league.

On the 20th the Mountaineers had to cut their roster per league regulations to 15 players and Joe made the cut. This in itself was a huge milestone because out of 50 or so rookies in the league, those playing their first year in the minors, only 1/3 of those would make it past the first roster cut. Joe was 2-2 so far and I think he had made a good impression in his first two starts. At 30 years old he was also one of the more mature and seasoned rookie pitchers around.

Playing on the road against the Scranton Miners on the 22nd of May Joe started in what would be the fastest game played at

Scranton in years and lasted only 1 hour and 19 minutes. Reading over Joes pitching summaries in the newspaper up until this point he seems to typically pitch a lot of short games. This leads me to believe that he works fast on the mound, the type of pitcher that is waiting on the batter to get situated in the box so he can deliver his pitch and not the other way around. This game was not only short but it was another low scoring affair and Scranton won it 3-2.

Playing in the minors was a lot different than what Joe was used to, not in the game itself but in the logistics surrounding it. In the semi-pros baseball wasn't his primary source of income. During the week he would go to work and after work go play a game, then return home. On the weekends he had time to spend with his family then get to the game. If he had an away game he would usually catch a train with the team that morning, go play the game, and catch a train home after the game. He also played for several teams at a time and if he wasn't needed in a game for the team he was signed with he would go play for another team. His day was centered on work and family and not necessarily baseball.

Now in the minors his day revolved around baseball because it was his primary job. Although he was committed to play for only one team he practiced every day and traveling was a team affair, which for away games usually involved getting to the ball field the day before and usually meant spending several days to get in a 3 to 4 game series. He was also living away from his family who were a 5 or 6 hour train ride away in

McKees Rocks. So life surrounding baseball had changed for Joe and I'm not sure how it affected his playing.

Playing a double header at Williamsport on Saturday the 30th the Mountaineers lost the morning game 5-1. In the afternoon game Joe went all 9 innings for a nice 7-3 win. Giving up 2 runs in the 2nd inning and another one in the 4th inning he held Williamsport scoreless and let the Hazleton bats do the work. Joe threw a strike out, had a hit, and drove in a run while holding Williamsport to 9 hits.

In an interesting game in Elmira, N.Y. the following day Joe wasn't playing when the Mountaineers took on the Colonels. With the Colonels ahead 1-0 going into the top of the 9th inning Hazleton was at bat. "Chief" Nason was on 2nd base when Bobby Nork came to the plate. He hit a single that drove Nason home. But the umpire didn't allow the tying run because he said that he had called time out before the hit so he could clear the crowd away from the base line. Upset Hazleton players crowded around the umpire demanding that he change his call. The umpire refused to change his decision and State Troopers had to be brought in to protect him from the players. The Mountaineers lost the game 1-0.

In the final game of their series with Elmira on the 1st of June Hazleton was losing 4-3 in the 5th inning when Joe came in relief and pitched the remaining 2-2/3 innings. The Mountaineers clawed their way back to a 7-7 tie going into the bottom of the 9th inning when Elmira scored the winning run. It was an 8-7 loss for Joe who had a hit and drove in a run.

The local papers were starting to grumble about how bad the Mountaineers were playing offensively and not hitting as well as they should be. On the other hand they were praising the pitching and saying how sad it was that such good pitching had to suffer due to a lack of good hitters on the club. As of the 5th of June Hazleton was in last place with a record of 10-18 and York was in 1st place at 16-11.

The Mountaineers were actually new to Hazleton and had just moved there from Syracuse, New York in 1929. Last year they had a losing season with a record of 63-76 and came in next to last place in the league. They fired last year's manager and hired Fitzgerald. When he took over this year he pretty much put an entirely new team on the field and the fans were hoping for a turn of fortune.

Joe gave a much needed boost to the Mountaineers when he picked up his 3rd win against the Williamsport Grays on the 5th. Playing at Bowman Park in Williamsport Joe held the Grays to 7 hits, threw 2 strikeouts, had 2 hits, drove in a run, and got the 4-1 win. This was his 3rd win against the Grays and he had them all at Bowman Park. In the three victory's he had only allowed the Grays 5 runs and 20 hits. With the win Joe started to get the nicknames "Big Joe" and the "Husky Hazleton" in the local papers.

Buhler Stadium had 2,200 fans come out on the 14th to spend a Sunday afternoon watching their home team take on Harrisburg. But they got behind 5-1 after 6-1/3 innings and Joe came in relief. It was a tough situation for Joe because the bases were loaded for him when he took the mound. The first batter he faced was Babe Fischer who hit it far over the right field fence for a grand slam homer scoring 4 runs and making it 9-1. Joe held the Senators scoreless for the remaining 3 innings but Hazleton lost 9-3. It was their sixth straight defeat.

They called it an "Iron Man" feat if you pitched back to back games in a double header, and that's what Joe took on against Harrisburg on the 17th. I'm surprised with his back that he would agree to pitch that many innings but he did, and he pitched well. The only problem was his team didn't help him with any offense. In the first game he lost 3-2 but kept the Senators to 8 hits and had 5 strikeouts. He also lost the 2nd game 1-0 and only allowed 2 hits and had a strikeout. It was 2 losses but it was also 18 innings of nicely pitched baseball.

Back on the mound on the 22nd of June Joe went against the Scranton Miners at Buhler Stadium in front of 600 hometown fans celebrating Lady's Night at the ballfield. Going against a left handed pitcher Joe stepped up to the plate in the 4th inning and tried batting left handed. After taking two weak swings at the ball, he switched over to his natural right handed batting stance and drilled the next pitch straight to the shortstop, unfortunately for an out. After 6 innings he was down 6-1, but in the bottom of the 8th inning the Mountaineers came roaring back and scored 5 runs to tie it at 6-6. Joe and the opposing starter came out after the 8th inning and the game stayed tied until it was called due to darkness after 10 innings.

After the game Joe had brought his family out on the train for an extended visit. In the short two months that Joe had arrived in Hazleton he had become very popular. When Harry Kratz the manager of the local amusement park, known as Hazle Park, heard that Joe had four young children he staged a special "Kiddies Day" and *"all of the little Semler's thought that they were as famous as their strong-armed dad when they hit every amusement in the park."*[30]

It was a long 3 hour game on Sunday the 28th that used up 7 pitchers as the Mountaineers hosted the Barons. Joe got the start in front of 2,500 fans but he only lasted 4-1/3 innings before being relieved. He was ahead 4-1, but after getting his first out in the 4th inning he started to slide. Three more Hazelton pitchers would take the mound before it was over. Wilkes-Barre threw 3 pitchers at Hazleton as they had their own hurling problems. But after 9 innings the Barons won 17-13. It was a high scoring affair with the Barons having a hit fest in the 5th inning scoring 7 runs and in the 7th inning scoring 8 runs. Hazleton had their own hot bats in the 6th inning scoring 6 runs. To add insult to injury Hazelton's star pitcher Jim Tennant, who they had just purchased for $10,000, was nailed trying to cover 1st base by a runner who went out of his way to collide with the pitcher. This game was definitely not a good day to be a pitcher.

Closing out June the Mountaineers took on the Miners in a double header at Scranton on the 31st. Another big crowd of 2,500 came out for the games and Hazleton won the first one 5-1. Joe started the second game and was up 3-0 after the 1st inning. But the Miners picked away at him and finally won 5-4.

It was another double header in front of another large crowd in Scranton on the 1st of July. The Mountaineers got skunked the 1st game 6-0. In the 2nd game Joe got the start and once again he had a 4-2 lead on the Miners going into the 5th inning. But the Miners tied it at 5-5 in the bottom of the 5th inning. Then he let them get ahead 6-5 in the bottom of the 6th inning. He was relieved in the 6th inning by Jim Tennant who took it all the way to the 13th inning when it was finally lost 7-6.

It wasn't getting any better when Williamsport paid a visit to Hazleton on the 4th of July for a double header. The Mountaineers dropped the 1st game 7-3. Joe once again got the start in the second game. He had proved that he could handle the Grays since he had already beaten them 3 times this season. But he must have been shaking his head asking where it all went wrong after they nailed him for 5 runs in the 1st inning without him even registering an out. He was relieved by Jim Tennant who must have also been shaking his head after they took him for 7 more runs in a 12-9 beating.

Finally in front of a hometown crowd at Buhler Stadium Joe gets a long awaited win. Playing the Binghamton Triplets on the 8th Joe pitched the first game of a double header. Getting a 3-0 lead by the 2nd inning Joe had some breathing room. The teams traded runs up to the 8th inning when Joe was still up 5-4. In the 9th inning he retired the Triplets in order and registered the win. Jim Tennant got the sweep in the second game shutting out the visitors 6-0.

But victory is short lived in the world of baseball. Traveling to Binghamton for a double header rematch on the 12th it was the Triplets turn to sweep the Mountaineers. Joe probably thought that pitching the first game last time was lucky so let's try it again. But the luck was gone and he got banged up for 5 runs and 10 hits in a 5-0 shutout. The second game didn't fare much better as Tom Ferrell was also shut out 2-0. So, the Triplets swept and shut out the Mountaineers.

Playing in Binghamton again on the 15th of July Vernon Kennedy got the start for the Mountaineers. He was holding a 3-1 lead going into the bottom of the 8th inning and had actually shut out the Triplets through 6 innings. But they gained a run in the 7th inning and he had two men on base and behind in the count to the batter when Joe was brought in. Joe didn't fare well and gave up 3 runs in the inning and the game was a 4-3 Mountaineer loss.

The Hazleton owners and fans had seen enough and heads had to roll. Hugh Fitzgerald with a record of 23-48 and holding down last place in the league all season was replaced with Jake Pitler. Hugh stayed on as a player and continued with Hazelton in the outfield but his brother Jerry was released. Jake Pitler had been playing in the minors since 1913 and had also played two years in the major leagues with the Pirates in 1917 and 18.

Getting some help from the Elmira Colonels on the 17th Joe was able to pull off a much needed win on the road. Pitching a steady game, getting some bat support from his teammates, and 6 Elmira errors gave Joe an 8-5 win. He was ahead 8-4 after 8 innings and was relieved in the 9th by Jim Tennant to hold down the last inning. He gave up a run but the win was secured.

Hazleton fans got their money's worth on the 21st when the Mountaineers hosted the York White Roses. Joe got the start and he pitched a solid game up until the 8th inning when York broke the scoreless game with 3 runs in the top of the inning. Hazleton came back in the bottom of the 9th inning for an exciting rally to score 3 runs themselves to tie the game. Tom Ferrell came in relief of Joe and held the game scoreless in the 10th inning. In the top of the 11th inning York put over a run to make it 4-3. In the bottom of the inning Alec Hooks drew a walk. Tom Ferrell was due up to bat but Jake Pitler chose to send Jim Tennant in to pinch-hit. Tennant sent the ball way over the left field fence for a 2 run homer and the 5-4 win!

It was another double header at home in front of 1,600 fans out for a Friday night on the 21st of July. The Harrisburg Senators were in town looking to break up Jake Pitler's 5 game winning streak since taking the helm of the Mountaineers. Ollie Carnegie slammed 2 homers in the first game but they came early and the game was tied going into the bottom of the 9th inning when Hazleton got the winning run over for a 7-6 victory and Pilter's sixth straight win. Joe got the start in the second game but only lasted 2-1/3 innings after getting behind 5-0. Newly acquired Floyd Van Pelt came in relief and held the visitors to only one more run. But even another homer by

Ollie Carnegie couldn't close the gap and the Senators won 6-3 and Jake Pilter's winning streak was ended.

On the road against York on the 27th Joe got the start. He was up 1-0 until the bottom of the 4th inning when York tied the game. In the bottom of the next inning he let them get 3 more runs that sealed the loss at 4-1. The Mountaineers were still in last place with a 29-52 record while the first place Barons were 48-34.

Joe got his last start of the month against Harrisburg on the 31st against their veteran pitcher Andy Rush. He had been a winning pitcher in the minors since 1914 and even pitched a few games in the majors with the Brooklyn Robins in 1925. He held Hazleton to 3 hits and had 9 strikeouts. Joe gave up 9 hits and had 5 strikeouts. And with tough pitching from Rush the Mountaineer bats were quiet and only scored a run. Joe gave up 6 runs in the 6-1 loss.

Just after this game the New York - Pennsylvania League banned the use of the "fast return" or "quick pitch" in which Andy Rush was famous for. This type of pitch is when the pitcher throws a fastball to the batter before he is set in the batter's box and ready to receive the pitch. Basically catching the batter off guard. You could move quick on the mound, like Joe and pitch a fast paced game, but you had to wait until the batter was set in the batter's box before you started your delivery.

As July ended there was a shake up with the Elmira Colonels who were currently in 7th place, just ahead of Hazleton. It was reported that they were in financial trouble and their uniforms were repossessed from the club house by creditors. It came out that they were in debt $26,000 and $3,000 of that was in player salaries. But at the last minute they were purchased by the St. Louis Cardinal's major league organization who were going to support them and place them in their farm system.

The Barons were in Hazleton on the 3rd of August for a double header in front of a crowd of 1,600. The Barons won the first game 10-4. Russell Haines started the second game which was slated for 7 innings. He had a comfortable 8-1 lead after 5 innings and gave the mound up to Joe to close the game. Joe let the Barons get 4 runs over in the 6th inning making it an 8-5 game and the fans got a little worried. It got shaky in the 9th inning when he had placed 2 men on base with 1 out. The next batter flied to right field for the 2nd out. When the right fielder threw the ball in it almost got past the catcher and a runner tried to make it home and score. But the runner was tagged out at the plate for the 3rd out. Hazleton won 8-5 and to the relief of the fans Joe didn't blow the game.

Hazleton hosted Scranton for a double header on the 6th of August. Joe started the early game and was up 2-0 after the 1st inning when Ollie Carnegie hit a 2 run homer. Hazelton picked up 2 more in the bottom of the 2nd to make it 4-2. Facing the opposing pitcher Carl Schoof in the top of the 4th inning Joe let him hit a 2 run homer to tie the game 4-4. In the top of the 5th inning the first batter hit a double off of Joe. The next batter, Chink Outen hit a homer making it 6-4. The next batter George McQuinn hit another homer to make it 7-4 and Joe threw his glove to the ground in disgust. In the top of the 6th inning he faced Chink Outen again and he hit a solo homer to make it 8-4. That was it for Joe and Vernon Kennedy came in relief. The game finally ended at 12-10 in favor of the Miners. They also won the second game 8-3 for the sweep.

I'm sure part of the problem Joe was having with getting hit so hard was that he had never faced the majority of these guys before. Playing in the Pittsburgh area for the past 10 years he had faced the majority of batters over and over and knew how to pitch to them. So I think it would just be a learning curve he would have to overcome here in the minors, hopefully before being released.

The Mountaineers traveled to take on the first place Wilkes-Barre Barons on the 12th in a double header. Joe hurled the first game in a nice pitching duel against June Green. He had been pitching in the minors since 1923 and played two years in the majors with the Philadelphia Phillies in 1928 and 29. The game was scoreless until the bottom of the 4th inning when the Barons scored 2 runs. But these were questionable after a close call at 3rd base was ruled in favor of the Barons. The dust up caused the entire Mountaineer bench to clear and swarm the field in protest. But the call stood. Later Hazleton manager Jake Pitler accused Green of using sand paper to scuff the ball and demanded that the umpire inspect his glove, which the umpire refused to do. In the 8th inning Joe led off with a double and then Hubie Fitzgerald singled sending Joe to 3rd base. The next two batters flied out. Ollie Carnegie then hit a hard line drive to the 3rd baseman, which he dropped. He immediately picked the ball up and threw it to 2nd base as Fitzgerald slid under the tag and Joe crossed home plate. But the umpire ruled Fitzgerald out at 2nd to end the inning. Once again the Hazleton bench cleared in protest to no avail. The Mountaineers lost the game 2-0. The second game was a 7 inning affair and was just as testy as the first. Mountaineer center fielder Eddie Burke got into it with the umpire on a called third strike to end the inning. As Burke took up his position in center field the umpire ejected him from the game. Hazleton actually had this game won 4-0 going into the 6th inning and gave up 6 runs to lose it 6-4 and give the Barons the sweep.

You may have noticed that the term "center field" is starting to be used in the newspapers more and more, replacing the term middle field.

Playing on the road in Scranton on the 14th Morrie Wilson got the start for Hazleton in front of a crowd of 1,200. The Miners were up 4-2 going into the bottom of the 8th inning when Joe came in relief. He got taken for 4 runs and the Mountaineers lost 8-2. This was the last game between these two teams for this season and their records against each other was a tie at 11-11.

Getting a start in the first game of a double header against the Elmira Colonels on the 17th Joe needed a good win in front of the hometown fans. He didn't disappoint them and his pitching performance was said to be the best of any Mountaineer so far this season. He forced the Colonels to retire in order except in the 4th inning. He only allowed 2 hits, had 6 strikeouts, and no walks. And as Joe walked off the field at the end of the 2-1 win the crowd broke out into a tremendous applause! Hazleton also won the second game 4-2 and for the first time since May 23rd they were no longer in last place in the league.

The following day the Mountaineers once again took on the Colonels in a double header at home and Joe got his second win in as many days. Morrie Willson took the mound in the first game but after getting hit hard in the 2nd inning Joe came in relief. Joe held the Colonels scoreless for the next 6 innings. Add in the scoreless 5 innings from yesterday and he had 11 scoreless innings against Elmira. Joe went on to win the game 9-5. The Mountaineers unfortunately didn't pick up the sweep again and lost the night cap 10-6.

The second place Williamsport Grays came to town for a double header on the 23rd and 1,300 fans came out for the action. Joe went against Red Parkes in the first game. Hazleton jumped out to a 4-0 lead in the 1st inning but the Grays slowly creeped up on the Mountaineers. In the 9th inning with Hazleton up 4-3 and with a runner on 3rd base Jim Tennant relived Joe of the pitching duties. The game went into the 11th inning when the Grays won it 5-4. Williamsport also picked up the second game 7-5 for the sweep.

It was another close game and tough loss for Joe on the 28th when he faced the Binghamton Triplets on the road for a double header. Getting the start in the first game at Johnson Park the game was tied up at 4-4 after 6 innings. It stayed that way until the 9th inning when Binghamton picked up the winning run and the game ended 5-4. Morrie Willson pitched the night cap and did a splendid job shutting out the Triplets 2-0 and avoided the sweep.

Joe got a chance to shine on the 1st of September against the 1st place Harrisburg Senators at home in Buhler Stadium. He threw a 1 hit game and almost had a no-hit and no-run game if he had not been robbed of that honor after the umpire reversed his decision on a ball hit up the 3rd base line he initially ruled foul. After a heated protest from the Senators he reversed his decision. Either way Joe got a nice 7-1 win over the league leaders. In the papers they pretty much summed up that Joe was having a "hard-luck" season. They also gave him a sort of back handed compliment saying he had the most losses in the league but was the best pitcher on the Hazleton squad.

The long haired and bearded House of David traveling exhibition team came to Buhler Stadium on the 3rd of September and drew a crowd of 7,000. The stadium could only hold 4,000 so the fans formed human walls along the base lines and outfield. It was Hazleton's first night game thanks to the House of David who brought their own lighting equipment consisting of four trucks used to carry six sets of lights and one truck carrying an electrical generating plant. The famous baseball player Grover Cleveland Alexander, who was elected into the baseball Hall of Fame in 1938, was on hand and pitched part of the 8th inning. When he took the mound he was cheered by the fans. Vernon Kennedy got the start for the

Mountaineers and Joe played 1st base. It was a real fan pleaser especially when Hazleton won 3-1.

Getting back to pitching Joe and the Mountaineers hosted Williamsport on the 5th in a double header. Joe pitched the early game against Red Parkes and was ahead 3-1 after the 3rd inning. He cruised along for a nice 5-3 win. Tom Ferrell pitched the second game and won 4-3 for the sweep which knocked the Grays out of the playoffs.

Joe and Tom pitched another double header on the 9th at Eagle Park in York. An unusually large crowd were on hand to see York display some of their newly signed players. In the opener Joe went against Earl Johnson and held the White Roses to 5 hits, threw 2 strikeouts, and had a hit in a 4-3 win. Tom Ferrell didn't do as well in the late game and lost 5-0.

Travelling to Harrisburg the Mountaineers played the newly crowned league champions in a double header on the 12th. They had such a lead no one could catch them so they were declared the champions before the season had ended. A little over 1,700 fans showed up at Island Park to see their champion team. Morrie Willson took the early game for a 2-1 loss. Joe took the evening 7 inning game and pitched against three different pitchers as the Senators rotated in some of their rookies so that they could get some playing time. They eventually rotated in 19 players trying to give everyone some time on the field. It didn't bother Joe who only allowed them 6 hits, struck out 2, and won the game 7-4.

That was it for the 1931 season. The teams disbanded on Monday the 14th and the players headed home until next year. Hazleton finished in 7th place with a record of 57-82. Joe's pitching record was 12-17, pitching 245 innings and 80 strikeouts. And he was one of only a few pitchers to complete the "Iron Man" feat and pitch back to back games in a double header. Granted he lost both games, but only by a 1 run margin in each game. The 17 losses were the highest in the league, which he shared with 2 other pitchers. I don't think Joe was proud of that statistic but I'm sure he was happy to have made it through his first year in the minor leagues.

While back at home Joe got one more game in on the 10th of October. It was a community benefit game between the Shenango Pottery squad and a team fielded by Al Scarazzo. All the players and umpires donated their time for the charity event which was played in front of a large crowd at Centennial Field. General admission was .25 cents and patron tickets were $1.00. Joe was pitching for Al's team and Paul McCullough for the Shenango pottery team. I couldn't find out who won the game but it did bring in over $375 for the charity.

1932:

In mid-March the Pittsburgh Press published an article about how Joe was undergoing contract negotiations with Hazleton for this upcoming season. The latest was that Joe had requested $400 per month to play and was awaiting word back on his offer. The article also went on to describe how good of a player Joe was and how he was not properly played at

Hazleton last year. It stated that he was often pitched out of rotation and that even with a 12-17 record he appeared in 41 games in relief work. It also stated that he lost a lot of close games due to Hazleton's lack of bat support. Interestingly it goes on to say that Baltimore had made an offer to acquire Joe, but Hazleton turned the offer down. Baltimore wasn't a major league team at the time but it did play in the minors.[31]

On the 28th of March Jake Pitler traveled to Mckees Rocks to personally discuss the contract with Joe and it was announced after their meeting that Joe would play for Hazleton this year. The details of the contract were not specified but I would have to imagine he got his $400 per month salary or close to it. That's about $6,000 in 2020 money. The average player in the minors was making around $250 and each team had a salary cap of $4,500.

Hazleton was getting excited about fielding a team again. And the Mountaineers new owner Joe Dunn said *"The boys will be made to hustle and play their best or else look for a new job."*[32] And the New York - Pennsylvania league felt the same way, well at least about the hustle. In fact, at a meeting held by team owners it was decided to vote at the end of the year on which team displayed the most hustle. The winning team would be awarded $400 from the league treasury. With the new ownership of the Mountaineers also came a change in major league farm ownership. Hazleton would now be in the Boston Red Sox farm system.

JOE SEMLER.

Joe Semler 1932[35]

There was also major work being done on Buhler Stadium with home plate being repositioned and the outfield fence being moved back 30 to 45 feet. This was needed due to the extremely large number of home runs hit there last year. Now the right field fence will be 400 feet from home plate and more in line with major league playing fields.

In early April Joe receive word that he would need to report to Mountaineer training camp at Berwick, Pa. on Friday the 15th. I found it interesting that the local Hazleton newspaper reported that an 18 year old from Reading, Pa. went to the Mountaineers club office at the American Bank Building in Hazleton and asked for a tryout. They told him if he was willing to pay for his expenses he could report on the 15th.

Berwick was only 20 miles from Hazleton and the 24 players that reported for spring training were lodged in the local hotel where the also took their meals. Practice was twice a day and consisted of two hour workouts on nearby Fowler Field. Just like last year they would be travelling back and forth to Hazleton playing exhibition games until their scheduled opener against Williamsport on the 3rd of May.

Probably the best exhibition game was when the Mountaineers hosted the Homestead Grays at Buhler Stadium on the 26th of April. Joe of course got the start against George Britt and he held the Grays scoreless for 6 innings before Tom Ferrell relieved him. Ferrell gave up 5 runs in the 9th inning and almost lost it. But Hazleton's Pat Reagan hit a 2 run homer in the bottom of the 9th inning for a 6-5 win.

As the Hazleton club prepared to start the 1932 season there were only 5 members returning from last year's squad and three of them were pitchers. So there was a lot of optimism that this was going to be a better season than last year. I don't think Joe liked being away from his family last year and just before the season started he rented a dwelling on North

Wyoming Street and moved them out to Hazleton. It wasn't a permanent move for them but just a summer rental while he was playing ball. When the season was over they would move back to their house in McKees Rocks.

After the opening day parade and ceremonies Joe got the start in the home opener against the Williamsport Grays on the 3rd of May in front of 2,000 excited fans. He was going up against the Grays Red Parkes who was their most reliable pitcher. The Mountaineers bats got Joe ahead 2-1 after the 1st inning. Then in the top of the 3rd inning the Grays scored a run to tie the game at 2-2 and Joe loaded the bases. A sensational one handed grab by 3rd baseman Jimmy Geygan made the third out and Joe got out of a tight spot. It was said that Joe wasn't his steady self during this game but he went on to hold the Grays scoreless for the next 6 innings while the Mountaineers picked up another run to give them the 3-2 win.

To celebrate opening day the Hazleton area merchants provided prizes to the players for different accomplishments. Like every player who got a hit in the game received a pair of socks from Eugene Jacobs Shirt Shop. I found the most interesting prize to be a carton of cigarettes that were presented to Roy Hutson for making the first run. Just what every athlete needed, a carton of cigarettes!

It was Lady's Day at Buhler Stadium on the 13th and all lady's got into the game for free. They helped make up the 1,500 fans that turned out to see Joe take on the Wilkes-Barre Barons. The Hazleton bats once again got Joe out to a comfortable 7-0 lead after 3 innings and Joe did the rest. Fanning 7, getting 2 hits, and scoring a run he led the way to a Mountaineer 10-6 win. It was their 5th straight win and they were comfortably sitting in 2nd place with an 8-1 record. After the 7th inning with Hazleton up 10-3 one of the Mountaineer fans had a bit of fun with the Barons manager. The fan presented the manager with a box. Not wanting to open it for fear of it being a prank the manager asked the umpire to open it, which he did. Inside was a dozen red roses with a note saying *"wishing you a speedy recover"* in reference to the impending Baron loss. After losing the game the manager graciously presented some of the ladies in the stands with red roses.

Heading to Scranton on the 17th to take on the Miners Si Slaalien got the start for the Mountaineers. The game came down to the bottom of the 9th inning with Hazleton up 11-7. Slaalien gave up 2 runs to make it 11-9 and with 2 men on base and 1 out Joe came in relief. Joe got the next two batters out on pop up's and secured the 11-9 win.

Joe got another start against Wilkes-Barre in a Thursday afternoon matchup on the 19th. He was pitching against Elmer "Pop" Knetzer who was a veteran pitcher who had pitched from 1909 to 1917 in the major leagues before shifting back to the minors. At 46 years old and still pitching he earned the nickname "Pop." The game was a 1-1 tie going into the bottom of the 2nd inning when the Mountaineers 2nd baseman dropped an easy pop up allowing 2 runs to score giving the Barons a 3-1 lead. The game stayed close and ended in a Baron 5-4 win. The loss was only one of 3 so far this year and the Mountaineers were holding on to 1st place with a 12-3 record.

It was the wrong day to be a Mountaineer pitcher when Binghamton came to town on the 23rd. The first batter Joe faced hit a leadoff home run and it didn't end there. He gave up 5 more runs before being relieved after only pitching 2/3's of the 1st inning. Down 6-0 Si Slaalien came in and gave up 2 more runs in his 4-1/3 innings of work before being relieved by Red Bates. He was nailed for 7 runs in his 2-1/3 innings and was finally relieved by Bill Droll who pitched the last 1-2/3 innings. After all that the Triplets had amassed a 16-4 win.

The Triplets must have had Joe's number because they banged him up again the following day. Getting the start again Joe lasted a bit longer than yesterday, but not much. After 3-2/3 innings Joe had given up 5 runs. Joe left 2 men on base when Tom Ferrell came in relief and the first batter he faced drove them in. After that things quieted down. But the Mountaineers bats were also quiet and they were handed a 7-1 loss. After starting out with a nice 2-0 record Joe was now 2-3 after tangling with the Triplets.

Taking on Williamsport in a double header at home on the 30th of May Bill Droll got the start. After getting behind 5-3 Joe came in to relieve him in the 5th inning. He gave up 4 more runs and the Mountaineer bats were once again quiet in a 9-4 loss. In the second game Tom Ferrell pitched the entire game for Hazleton but couldn't pull out the win and the Grays took it

7-3 for the sweep. After the double loss Hazleton was 19-9 and still in 1st place, but just 1 game ahead of Harrisburg.

Could it get any worse against the Triplets? Well, I know this game summary is going to sound a lot like the game on the 23rd of last month but it is in fact a different game. Traveling to Binghamton on the 1st of June Joe got the start and the Triplets scored 6 runs in the 1st inning. With only 1 out and down 6-0 Si Slaalien relieved Joe and gave up 3 more runs before he could get the Mountaineers out of the 1st inning. Si lasted 2 more innings before being relieved by Bill Droll who took the game to the end. When it was finally over the Triplets had racked up a 12-7 win.

The Harrisburg Senators came to Hazleton on the 5th and Joe was hoping his luck would change with them. Over 3,000 fans came out to see the two teams who were tied for first place in the league. Joe got the start and the Senators hit him for 4 runs in the 1st inning. Staying in the game they got 6 more runs off of him in the 2nd inning! With 2 outs Bill Droll came in relief and Joe went to the showers. Surprisingly the game was actually close after that and the Mountaineers came back to only let the Senators win by 1 run in a 15-14 game. Interestingly Bill Droll hit an inside the park solo homer in the 5th inning when he drove the ball into left center field right between the two outfielders who couldn't catch up with it as it rolled to the fence.

A lot changes in four days and for Joe it was all good. Back in 1st place Hazleton traveled to York to try and gain a few games on the White Roses who were currently in 2nd place. A crowd of 1,500 turned out to Eagle Park to watch the game. Joe got the start and held the home team scoreless and only allowed 3 hits in a nicely pitched 1-0 shutout.

Playing York again on the 16th Joe got the start in front of a light crowd of 500 at Buhler Stadium. Getting behind 5-4 Joe was relieved in the 4th by Si Slaatien. But after only 1 more inning the game was called due to rain and York got the 5-4 win. The loss unfortunately knocked Hazleton out of 1st place.

Dropping down to 4th place by the 22nd Hazleton traveled to Wilkes-Barre. Joe had another rocky 1st inning serving up a curve ball that got smacked for a 3 run homer. But after that he settled down and only gave up 2 more runs the rest of the game. The Mountaineer bats were quiet and the game ended 5-1 and gave Hazleton their 5th straight loss. After the loss the Mountaineers announced that they had signed two left handed pitchers and were going to place them on the roster for a try out period. In order to do that they needed to remove two pitchers so they would maintain their 15 player roster cap. So Joe and Hickey were placed on the suspended list for 5 days. It's actually not a bad position to be in for Joe because his pitching arm had been sore since early May and he hadn't had a chance to rest it.

Making his mound comeback on the 28th the Mountaineers were hosting Wilkes-Barre. It was also Booster Day and 1,400 fans came out for the festivities. Joe got behind 7-4 after giving up 2 homers and a triple in the 5th inning and Walter Ramsey, one of the new lefty's, came in to relieve Joe. He held the Barons scoreless in the top of the 6th inning and the Mountaineers scored 4 runs in the bottom of the 6th to take the lead at 8-7. Ramsey held the Barons scoreless for the win. The victory moved Hazleton up to 3rd place.

Over the July 4th weekend the Mountaineers were catching up on rained out games from June and squeezing in as many games as they could. On Saturday at home Walter Ramsey got the start against Scranton but got behind 6-3 after 5 innings. Joe came in and held the Miners scoreless for the remaining 4 innings while the Mountaineer bats got hot and scored 5 runs for an 8-6 win. Hazleton went on to lose the Sunday game against the Miners and split a double header with Williamsport on Monday the 4th at Bowman Park.

Due to a nationwide Amusement Tax taking effect the league decided not to raise their admission prices as anticipated but would absorb the costs with some slight modifications. General admission would be .50 cents for bleacher seats, .75 cents for grand stand seats, and $1.10 for box seats. Ladies will have to pay .10 cents at the gate now on Lady's Day and .25 cents on all other days.

Just after the July 4th series it's announced that Joe has been bought by the Scranton Miners. With a record of 5-7 he wasn't off to a great start and the local Hazleton papers didn't cover his departure negatively. In fact I got the impression that Joe was well liked by the press in Hazleton and they covered him over the past year and a half very fairly. He was also a fan favorite and it was reported that he would be missed and always welcomed back. It wasn't like leaving a team was anything unusual and players moved around constantly. It was the nature of the game to be traded or sold as clubs tried to get the right players in their lineup. So, Joe packed his bags, leaving his family in Hazleton[32], and headed 40 miles north to Scranton.

Scranton Miners

1932

It didn't take long for Joe to get a start as a Miner and he suited up on the 6th of July to take on Earl Johnson and the York squad at Eagle Park. After pitching 7 innings he was behind 3-1 and was relieved by McLaughlin who got the Miners ahead 4-3, but York came back to win it in the 9th inning 5-4. It was actually a mess in the bottom of the 9th for Scranton. Their 1st and 3rd baseman were ejected for arguing a close call at 1st base that sided with York. Then the bases got loaded and the winning run was walked in.

When Joe left Hazleton they were in 4th place and when he arrived in Scranton the Miners were in 7th place. The team was definitely having some difficulties and the fans were not happy with their manager Bill Clymer.

Scranton wasn't the only team facing problems. The Depression was starting to affect the entire league and the owners were complaining about low revenue due to low fan turn out. Binghamton was on the verge of bankruptcy but hanging on. And Harrisburg was facing bankruptcy but announced it had just been bought out and the new owners were promising to keep the team on the New York – Pennsylvania League.

Getting the start on the 10th Joe was under a new manager, Bob Shawkey, who was taking over a club now in last place. It was Joe's first start at home in Crystal Garden Stadium and 3,000 fans came out to see their new pitcher take on the Harrisburg Senators. Joe was behind 5-2 and was relieved by Floyd Olds after 2-1/3 innings. But the Miners came back to tie it right after Joe came out in the bottom of the 3rd inning and won the game 12-9.

Joe's new manager Bob Shawkey was a pretty big deal in baseball. He had played in the major leagues from 1913-1927 and most of that time he was pitching for the New York Yankees. He was on the Yankees squad when they won the World Series in 1923 and 1927 and managed them in 1930. And when Scranton brought him in to relieve Bill Clymer they also released 4 players in a major act of house cleaning.

Scranton hosted York on the 13th and Red Sweeny got the start and he played a part in the York manager and 1st baseman getting tossed from the game for arguing strikes with the umpire. The White Roses eventually got the last laugh when they got ahead of him by a score of 8-5 after 4-2/3 innings and Martin Gates came in relief. He only lasted 1-1/3 innings before he was relieved by Joe. When Joe took the mound he was behind 10-5. He let York get 2 more runs but Scranton also scored 2 more for a 12-7 York win.

After the game Scranton announced that Joe was being released from the team and he had been signed by York. Scranton had just signed a new pitcher by the name of George Kirsch from the International League and they needed to unload a pitcher to make room for him. York signed Joe because Earl Johnson had just suffered a leg injury and they needed someone to fill in for him. It was actually a better move for Joe because York was currently in 2nd place with a record of 40-32 and Scranton was way back in 7th place.

York White Roses

1932

Joe got his first start with York on the 16th in a double header on the road against Wilkes-Barre. A crowd of 3,000 came out to see their 1st place Barons. Claude Satterfield got the start for York in the early 9 inning contest and pitched a nice 3-2 win. In the later 7 inning game Joe got the start against the league's best left hander Johnnie Milligan. Joe held the home team to 5 hits and threw 2 strikeouts but Milligan was a bit better only allowing 3 hits and throwing 3 strike outs. The Barons won 2-1.

Getting a go at the Mountaineers for the first time since leaving them Joe got the start at Eagle Park on the 19th of July. Going into the game York was in 3rd place and Hazleton was in 4th place. Joe held the visitors to 8 hits and fanned 8 in a 4-1 win. He gave up the only run in the 3rd inning and pitched a solid game.

It was Joe's second start on the 23rd of July. In front of 800 fans at Island Park he was going against June Green and the Harrisburg Senators. York got him out ahead by a run in the top of the 1st inning but by the end of the 3rd inning it was tied 2-2. Then the White Roses scored 3 more runs in the top of the 4th inning to make it 5-3. Joe gave up a run in the bottom of the 9th inning but held on to the 5-3 win. It was his second in a row since joining York. The White Roses had swept their series with the Senators and were now in 2nd place.

Travelling to Williamsport on the 28th Joe got the start against Red Parkes. It was the Grays "Booster Night" at Bowman Park and 2,000 fans were on hand for the game. Joe held the Grays scoreless until the bottom of the 5th inning when they took a 2-1 lead. Joe came out after the 8th inning and Claude Satterfield came in. The game was tied 3-3 in the 9th inning and the Grays put over the winning run in the 10th inning to end it 4-3. Claude got the loss and Joe was still 2-1.

Closing out July York took on the Elmira Red Wings (previously the Colonels) in a double header on the 31st. York swept the series at home in front of 2,500 jubilant fans. Jim Pattison won the opener 9-3 and Joe pitched the nightcap holding the visitors to 5 hits in an 11-5 beating. The 1st place Wilkes-Barre Barons were also swept and York was closing in on 1st place.

Getting the start at home in Eagle Park on the 4th of August Joe took on the Triplets. Joe has had a tough time with the Triplets the past year and a half and today was no different. He actually pitched a pretty good game and had 7 strikeouts. But a lack of run support and timely hitting by Binghamton gave them the 5-3 win. The loss gave the Barons a full game lead ahead of York.

Traveling to Elmira for a double header on the 7th of August York had several new players in their lineup as they tried to keep up with the Barons. The deadline to add new players was coming up on the 12th so York was making their pennant run roster adjustments. The early game went to York when Jimmy Brett took the mound for a 7-4 win. Joe got the night cap duties and the Red Wings beat him 7-0. The loss dropped the White Roses to 3rd place and 4 players along with their manager were released in a team shakeup. Their new manager Frankie Dessau was a long time minor and major league player and manager who had managed the White Roses before.

It was another Triplet game on the 12th and Binghamton had that Triplet jinx working on Jim Brett. He was the starting pitcher and cruising along with 14 strikeouts and ahead 7-0 going into the bottom of the 8th inning. Then the Triplets scored 4 runs to make it 7-4. Okay not a problem, there is only one more inning to get through. Well in the bottom of the 9th inning they scored 2 more to make it 7-6 and the tying run was on base. That was enough for Jim, and Joe came in relief. Joe got the next batter to hit into a double play to end the game and secure the 7-6 win! Maybe the Triplet jinx had been broken.

The 3rd place White Roses traveled to play the 4th place Mountaineers on the 14th in a double header. Jim Pattison got the start in the first game and had a 5-4 lead going into the bottom of the 9th inning. Hazleton got another run to tie the game at 5-5 and had 2 men on base. Joe came in and they walked the first batter to load the bases. The next batter hit a line drive scoring the winning run. Bill Simmon got the start in the evening game but after giving up 5 runs in the 1st inning Joe came in relief. He gave up 6 more in an 11-7 loss and a sweep by the Mountaineers. The double loss didn't change the league standings because York was several games ahead of Hazleton going into this series.

It was a wild game when the league leading Wilkes-Barre Barons came to York on the 17th. Bill Simmon got the start and after 2-1/3 innings of wild pitching and down 4-1 Joe came in with runners on 1st and 3rd. The first batter hit a slow grounder to Joe and he trapped the runner on 3rd in a run-down trying to make it home. As Joe gave chase the runner fell down and Joe tripped over him, injuring himself. He wanted to stay in the game although he was obviously in great pain. His next pitch was sent over the fence for a 3 run homer making it a 7-1 game and Joe came out and Jimmy Brett came in. Brett, with his side arm submarine style of pitching, shut out the Barons for the remainder of game and the White Roses came back to win it 8-7.

Joe was taken for x-rays for a suspected cracked rib. But after being examined at York Hospital he was found to have fractured the little finger on his left hand just below the 3rd joint. His ribs weren't broken and just sore. In a way he was lucky it wasn't his throwing hand just his catching hand. But the injury ended the season for Joe and he packed up his family in Hazleton at the end of August and moved back to McKees Rocks for the off season. Joe was expected to return to York next year and he was on their reserve list of players to be re-signed.

The season ended September 14th and Joe officially had a record of 7-10 with Hazleton, Scranton, and York. Wilkes-Barre won the league pennant with a record of 76-61, York came in 3rd with a record of 72-66, Scranton came in 4th with a record of 72-68, and Hazleton came in 6th with a record of 62-72.

Joes hand was ready to pitch on the 23rd of September when he pitched a game with the Minor League All-Stars back in Pittsburgh. Dormont's manager Billy Fuchs had compiled a team of local minor league stars to include Joe, Ollie Carnegie, Elmer Knetzer, Dick Goldberg and others. They would go up against the Pittsburgh Crawford's from the Negro League. They had just formed as a team in 1931 and had some of the elite black players of the time playing for them. Guys like Josh Gibson, Satchel Paige and Jud Wilson.

The game was played at Greenlee Field in the Hill District of Pittsburgh where the Crawford's owner, Gus Greenlee, had just built a stadium. Joe got the start and pitched most of the game before giving his hand a rest. By all indications this was his first pitching outing since breaking his finger. The All-Stars lost 11-4 but Joe at least had 3 strikeouts.

Wilkes-Barre Barons
1933 to 1934

In mid-April the local Pittsburgh papers were reporting that Joe had signed with the local City league and was going to be playing for the Book Shoe team back in the semi-pros. And on the 9th of May Joe confirmed that he had turned down a contract offer to play back in the New York - Pennsylvania League and was going to pitch for the Book Shoe club. He was having a salary dispute with York and had refused to report to spring training until his contract was renegotiated.[34]

Opening day for Book Shoe was on the 12th of May at Homewood. Bimmy Steele took the mound for Book Shoe and Al "Curly" Semler took left field for Homewood. Al hit a double but Book Shoe won the game 4-0. Joe didn't play and watched his brother from the bull pen.

Playing Dormont on the 19th Joe got the start for Book Shoe and Leo Carroll started for Dormont. With the game tied at 6-6 after 4 innings Joe was relieved by Abe Martin and Leo by Les Richards. They took the game to the end which finished in a 9-6 Dormont victory.

I think Joe enjoyed playing with his old mates again. I mean just writing the last couple of paragraphs has been sort of reminiscent of all the games Joe had played with these guys and these teams.

Taking on the J.L. Thomas club at home on the 1st of June Abe Martin got the start for Book Shoe. He pitched a fine game getting a 6-0 lead after 3 innings. But after the 6th inning Thomas had closed the gap to 6-5 and Joe came in relief. He held them off for a 9-6 win. Abe had 7 strikeouts and Joe 3. The win kept them tied in 1st place with Dormont with a record of 7-2.

With Book Shoe in 2nd place in the City League Joe decides to leave them and head back to the minors. He was not able to come to an agreement with York and they released him. He then accepted an offer from Wilkes-Barre back in the New York – Pennsylvania League. Due to the Depression the league had lowered its salary cap down to $2,800 a month so I don't think he would have been offered anywhere near the $400 he had received with Hazleton in 1931. His contract amount was never mentioned but it had to be higher than what he was getting playing in the semi-pros. A big influence for him to join Wilkes-Barre had to be that his very close friend

Elmer Yoter had just taken over managing and playing 3rd base for the Barons.

The Barons were currently in 3rd place with a record of 25-18 and chasing 1st place Scranton. The New York – Pennsylvania League had also moved up to the Class-A minor leagues and had dropped Hazleton and added Reading this year.

Joe didn't waste any time getting on the Wilkes-Barre squad and joined them on the 14th while they were on the road at Binghamton. He was actually hired to replace Merle "Lefty" Settlemire who was on the disabled list due to a strained leg muscle. Joe would be on a 10 day probation period and the Barons could release him if they didn't like the way he performed.

Two days later on the 16th Joe was on the mound in Elmira taking on the Red Wings. He shut out the home team the first 5 innings and they finally got 2 runs off of him in the bottom of the 6th inning to make it a 5-2 game. He got himself a hit in the top of the 8th inning and was batted in to make it 6-2. Joe came out in the 9th inning and was relieved by Nick Harrison who gave up 1 more run. But the win was secured for Joe and he got his first Baron victory. It also put the Barons in 2nd place just a game behind Scranton.

The Barons were in Reading to take on the Red Sox on the 18th for a double header. In the first game the Barons 1st baseman Harold Grant broke a bone in his ankle in the 8th inning when he caught it wrong on the bag at 2nd base running out a hit. Joe came in to replace him and the Barons lost 7-6. In the second game Joe played 1st base again in a 15-10 Baron victory. Joe went hitless in 4 at bats.

Playing the Red Sox in Reading again on the 20th Joe took the mound. He held the home team scoreless through 6 innings. They finally got a run in the 7th inning to make it a 3-1 game. It looked like Joe had it all sewn up with a 4-1 lead going into the bottom of the 9th inning when the game got exciting. The first batter Joe faced singled, the second flied out, and the third hit a 2 run homer to make it a 4-3 game. I'm sure Joe was getting a bit nervous at this point. The next two batters singled and the third hit a soft grounder to Joe for the easy put out at 1st base. Now with runners on 2nd and 3rd base with 2 outs he faced probably the most important batter of the game. Joe made his delivery and the batter grounded out to the 2nd baseman to end the game. Joe got out of a jam and got the 4-3 win.

Taking the mound on the 25th at Bowman Park Joe faced off against the Grays. Both teams were hot in the 1st inning and it was 3-2 in favor of the Barons going into the 2nd inning. The game slowed down from there and Joe went on to win it 6-4.

Wilkes-Barre was still a game behind Scranton and Lefty Settlemire who had been on the disabled list was brought back to the roster. To make room for him a pitcher had to go and Nick Harrison was released. Harrison had been with the Barons since the start of the year and a fan favorite. There were speculations in the paper as to why he was released and Joe and another pitcher by the name of Eddie "Cole"

Koslowski were retained. Elmer Yoter said it came down to the roster cap and that Joe and Eddie were considered rookies and the team had to maintain a certain number of rookies on the roster. So, Joe made it past his 10 day probation and stayed on the roster. I'm sure starting out with 3 wins, being a versatile pitcher, and also being able to play 1st base helped in securing his place on the team.

It was Booster Day for the Barons on the 28th and they hoisted last year's league winning pennant up the flag pole. A crowd of 2,500 fans came out to Artillery Park to watch their team, who had just inched into 1st place, take on the Grays. Bud Shaney got the start for the Barons but after getting behind 4-1 in the middle of the 4th inning Joe came in relief. Joe gave up 2 more runs in the 6-3 loss which dropped the Barons back to 2nd place.

July just wasn't starting out the way the Barons would have liked. Traveling 100 miles by bus to Elmira, New York they suited up and the game was called due to rain. So they loaded back up on the bus for another 100 mile trip back to Wilkes-Barre for a double header with Williamsport in which they lost both games. Not only were they out of the neck and neck match up with Scranton for 1st place but they had fallen all the way to 3rd place behind 2nd place Scranton and 1st place Binghamton.

Joe's 3 game winning streak also came to an end when the Barons hosted Scranton on the 3rd of July. Joe got the start against Bill Frazier who put on a pitching show holding the

Barons to 3 hits in a 5-0 shutout. Joe wasn't doing too badly and it was 4-0 when he came out after 8 innings. Bud Shaney pitched the last inning and gave up the final run for the 5-0 shutout loss.

It didn't take Joe long to get another win and get Wilkes-Barre moving in the right direction. Traveling to Harrisburg to take on the Senators Joe initially faced Hal Conklin until the 7th inning when he was relieved by Al Reitz. The Senators were ahead 3-0 going into the top of the 6th inning when the Barons woke up and scored in each of the next three innings to take a 7-4 win. Wilkes-Barre was still in 3rd place with a 38-31 record.

Joe had the Senators number and on the 10th handed them their worst loss of the year. And the boys from Harrisburg were not happy about the beating especially after winning their last 20 out of 26 games. To add insult to injury Frank Parenti, the Barons 2nd baseman, stole home for the 3rd time this year in the 6th inning. As the Senators catcher threw the ball to the pitcher, Parenti raced home. The pitcher was so surprised at the steal attempt that he dropped the ball! Joe went the entire 9 innings in the 13-2 win. The victory put the Barons in 2nd place behind Binghamton.

As the Barons got on a roll the league itself was running into some problems as the Depression dragged on. With probably the best month to play baseball teams were having a tough time drawing crowds. It was tossed around last month at an owners meeting that general admission should be lowered to .40 cents from the current .50 cents to attract more people, but the idea didn't get owner approval. Now there were rumors that Williamsport wanted to cash out and may sell to Hazleton who was without a team. And York said that they may have to fold due to financial troubles and that they still owed their players some of their June salaries. Even Wilkes-Barre who had great fan support was only drawing crowds as low as 200 fans in several games this month.

As if things couldn't get worse the Barons drop a double header to Harrisburg who were obviously looking for some revenge. The double loss dropped Wilkes-Barre out of 2nd place and put the Senators right on their heels in 4th place. Lefty Settlemire lost the first game 2-1 and Earl Johnson the second game 9-5.

With the Barons in a three way battle for 1st place Joe took the mound against Elmira's Bob Klinger at Artillery Park on the 17th. The Red Wings took a 1-0 lead in the top of the 4th inning and the Barons tied it in the bottom of the 7th inning. It went all the way until the 11th inning with the same starting pitchers when Elmira finally got a run past Joe and won 2-1.

Needing to gain some ground on the league leading Triplets Joe took the mound against Floyd Olds on the 21st. Playing at Artillery Park the Barons jumped out to a 1-0 lead in the 1st inning. Binghamton scored 3 runs in the top of the 4th inning to make it 3-1. Then in the bottom of the 6th inning with 2 outs the Barons catcher, Uzmann, walked. Then Joe spanked a single out to center. Tice, the Barons center fielder got a hit that scored Uzmann and put Joe on 3rd base. Parenti walked then Joe Dwyer hit a long drive that hit the fence and drove in Joe, Tice, and Parenti to make it 5-3. The Triplets got one more run in the top of the 8th inning and it ended 5-4. Joe held Binghamton to only 4 hits and the victory cut the Triplets lead to only 3-1/2 games ahead of the Barons in 3rd place. Joe was now 6-2 since joining the Barons and the team's second best pitcher behind Earl Johnson who was 13-5.

By the 27th the Barons were in 2nd place and needed a win against 1st place Binghamton. Joe got the start against Jimmy Densmore at Johnson Park. Densmore was a young hurler who would go on and have a 20 game winning season this year and today he would rack up number 18. Joe got behind 5-1 after 6 innings and Lefty Settlemire came in relief for the remaining 3 innings. He gave up another run and the Triplets won 6-2.

The Barons traveled to Reading on the 30th for a double header. Lefty Settlemire got the start in the first game and never made it out of the 1st inning before Joe had to come in relief down 4-0 with runners on base and 2 outs. Joe ended up giving up a run but finally ended the 1st inning behind 5-0. He ended up giving them 4 more runs before it was over and they fell 9-4. Bud Shaney got the start in the second game and the Red Sox won that one 6-3 for the sweep. The two losses dropped Wilkes-Barre down to 3rd place behind Scranton and 1st place Binghamton.

The Red Sox came to Wilkes-Barre on the 4th of August and the Barons sent Joe to the mound against Justin McLaughlin.

He was bouncing back and forth between the major league Red Sox and the minor league team. Joe and Justin duked it out in a 1-1 tie into the 10th inning when a wild throw by Elmer Yoter gave up the winning run and Joe lost 2-1. In the second game Bud Shaney got the start and lost the game 5-2. The only thing that made the fans happy about this double header was the fact that the Barons had lowered the general admission price to .40 cents for the game.

Trying to strengthen his bullpen and get back into the running for 1st place Elmer Yoter released Eddie "Cole" Koslowski and Bud Shaney. Shaney was a fan favorite and he was immediately signed by Scranton. To take their place the Barons signed Joe Gilvery who is a 6 foot, 175 pound left hander and was playing for the Dayton Ducks in the Central League. Last year he was the 3rd best pitcher in the league with a record of 18-8.

Williamsport came to Wilkes-Barre on the 9th of August for a four game series and Joe got the start of the first game in front of 500 fans. The Barons jumped out to a 5-0 lead at the end of 3 innings and Joe held the Grays scoreless until the top of the 6th inning when he gave up 2 runs to make it 5-2. Holding them scoreless in the top of the 7th inning Lefty Settlemire came in with a fresh arm to close the game. But he gave up 2 runs in the 8th inning and 4 runs in the 9th inning to blow the win and hand the Grays a 9-5 victory. The loss dropped the Barons into 4th place.

Traveling to Elmira on the 13th for a double header Joe took the mound in the early game against Bob Klinger in a pitching duel. The game was scoreless after 5 innings when it was called due to rain. Joe held the Red Wings to 3 hits and threw 2 strikeouts while Klinger only gave up 4 hits and struck out 5. The late game was cancelled due to the rain and the Barons headed home to take on York.

Getting back home to play York in a double header on the 15th Earl Johnson took the mound in the early game and pitched a nice 5-1 win. Joe took the evening game against Lefty George and it was the Joe Semler show. He only allowed 2 hits, struck out 1, and shut out the White Roses 4-0. It was the 6th straight win for the Barons and Joes 7th win on the year. The sweep put them back in 3rd place.

Playing a double header with the Senators on the 18th at Island Park in front of 1,000 fans Joe got the start in the early game against Charlie Eckert. Joe had his curve ball working and held Harrisburg scoreless through 8 innings while the Barons piled up a 6-0 lead. Finally in the bottom of the 9th inning the Senators rallied but it was too little and the Barons won 6-4. Earl Johnston pitched the late game and won it 3-1 for the sweep. Just for the record Joe had pitched 20 consecutive scoreless innings until he finally gave up a run in the 9th inning of the first game.

Heading up to a double header in Elmira on the 27th Joe pitched the early game against Wetherhill. Joe went 9 innings without giving up a run and limited the Red Wings to 6 hits and threw 4 strikeouts as he took a 2-0 win. Joe Gilvery started the late game and was eventually relieved by Lefty Settlmire in a 7-1 loss. The series left the Barons in 3rd place with a record of 65-57.

Traveling to Binghamton on the 31st the Barons played a double header against the 1st place Triplets. Joe got the start in the opener, which was working out really well for him here lately, against Ray White. Joe did a little of everything in the game getting a hit, driving in a run, striking out 2, and winning it 3-2. He did actually just about single handily win it. Not only with his pitching but in the top of the 9th inning his single drove in Jake Plummer for the winning run. Joe Gilvery took the night cap and lost it 7-1

Getting another crack at the Triplets at Artillery Park on the 2nd of September in front of 2,000 fans Fred Niggeling took the mound in the opener and lost a close 2-1 game. Earl Johnson was looking for his 20th win of the season in the evening game but in the 6th inning he let the Triplets catch up and tie it 3-3. Joe came in relief and held Binghamton scoreless until the Barons got a run to win it 4-3 giving Joe the victory. The series with the Triplets didn't change the Barons standing and they maintained 3rd place.

Joe got his 6th win in a row in front of a home town crowd of 1,500 fans who took a chance that the late game wouldn't be rained out like the game earlier in the day. Facing Johnny Milligan of Scranton Joe held the visitors to 1 run as he struck out 4 and pitched a nice 4-1 win. The victory placed Joe at 12-

4 so far this year and he had only allowed 13 runs in 67 innings.

The season was winding down and with only 4 games left in the season Joe pitched his last game on the 8th of September in a double header with Elmira. Playing on the road Fred Niggeling got the start in the first game and lost it 4-3. Joe was matched up against Charlie Eckert in the second game and the Barons got him out to a nice lead scoring 9 runs in the 3rd inning. Eckert was relieved and Joe went on to face two more pitchers as the Red Wings tried to catch up. But the game ended 9-3 and Joe ended the season with win number 13.

The season ended with Binghamton taking the 1st place pennant, Reading coming in 2nd, and Wilkes Barre 3rd with a record of 71-67. Joe won the pitching title with a record of 13-4, 60 strikeouts, and an ERA of 2.32. And Elmer Yoter set a league fielding record with 186 putouts and 305 assists.

The Barons had scheduled some exhibition games with local teams but cancelled them and the team disbanded on the 11th of September. Joe headed home to McKees Rocks and unlike in previous years he didn't get involved in any games back home. Oh, and Earl Johnson did get his 20 wins and finished the year with a record of 20-10 with an ERA of 2.85.

1934:

In March the Wilkes-Barre papers reported that Joe had re-signed with the Barons along with fellow pitchers Earl Johnson and Merle "Lefty" Settlemire. New additions were Al Reitz who played for Scranton last year and Charlie "Lefty" Willis from Class-B. Spring training started on the 16th of April and 60 players came out to try and make the team. Fifteen of those were trying out for pitcher so the competition to make the team was tough. And just because you had a contract didn't guarantee you a spot on the team.

Getting ready for the season the Barons primary roster was announced as follows: Joe Semler, Earl Johnson, Cy Turner Joe Jackym, and Al Reitz pitching; Joe Klinger, Guy Shatzer, and George Klinger catchers; Dick Goldberg 1st base; Frank Parenti 2nd base, Johnny "Bunny" Griffiths shortstop; Elmer Yoter 3rd base & manager; Joe Dwyer left field; Hubie Fitzgerald center field; and Jake Plummer right field.

There were some significant changes in the New York – Pennsylvania League for the 1934 season. First, the York White Roses had dropped out of the league and were replaced by the Hazleton Mountaineers who had been playing in the Independent League last year. And second, was the addition of a championship series at the end of the season. Previously the league champion was determined by the team with the best record at the end of the season. Now the season would be broken into two parts, a 1st half and a 2nd half. The 1st half would run from May 1st to July 4th and the 2nd half from July 5th to September 9th. The winner of the 1st and 2nd half would play a 7 game series to determine the league champion. As an incentive to win both halves the winning team was guaranteed $1,500, which would break down to $100 per player. And if there was a championship series the two teams would receive

75% of the gate revenue and the winning team would get 60% of that and the losers 40%.

Wilkes-Barre had their home opener against Scranton on the 2nd of May in front of 3,500 fans at Artillery Park. Joe took the mound and the Barons were looking for the second win of the season after Earl Johnson beat the Miners in their home opener the previous day. But it just wasn't Joe's day and after getting behind 4-0 after 6 innings Joe was relieved by Charlie "Lefty" Willis. The Barons ended up losing the game 6-3 and Joe started the year with his first loss.

Joe Klinger, Joe Semler, Joe Dwyer, and Dick Goldberg[36]

Joe got back on the mound against last year's champion Triplets in Wilkes-Barre on the 7th. He was facing Ray White and the two had a nice pitching duel going when Joe singled to drive in the tying run in the 3rd inning to make it 3-3. Then in the 8th inning it was tied 3-3 when Joe came out and Earl Johnson took the mound. He pitched until the 12th inning when the Barons finally got a run across to win it 4-3. The win placed the Barons in 1st place with a record of 5-1.

Traveling to Williamsport for a double header on the 12th Joe was up against Buddy Hearn, a veteran lefty, in the early game. It was scoreless until the bottom of the 4th inning when the Grays scored 2 runs to make it 2-0. The Barons picked up a run in the top of the 6th inning but the Grays answered back in the bottom of the 7th inning with 2 more runs to make it 4-1. Both teams picked up another run and the game ended in a 5-2 Gray victory. Joe Jackym got the start in the late game and won it for the Barons 3-1. He was a famous knuckle ball pitcher and had been recruited from Notre Dame where he played college baseball.

Hosting Williamsport on the 16th Lefty Willis got the start against Buddy Hearn. Willis was behind 4-3 in the top of the 8th inning when he gave up a run and loaded the bases with only 1 out. Joe came in relief and retired the next 2 batters to get out of the inning. But with 2 outs in the top of the 9th inning Joe gave up 3 runs before retiring the Grays who walked off with an 8-3 win.

It was already halfway through the month and Joe was 0-2 and hadn't picked up his first win. In fact he had the worst record on the team. Al Reitz had the best record in the league at 3-0, Charlie Willis had the third best in the league at 3-2. Joe Jockym was 2-0, and Earl Johnson was 2-2.

Hazleton came to Wilkes-Barre for a double header on the 20th and over 5,000 fans came out for a Sunday game at Artillery

Park to see their 1st place Barons. Joe took the mound in the early game which started out with a close play at the plate in the bottom of the 1st inning. The Barons center fielder Zach Smith was headed home and collided with the Hazleton catcher and they both tumbled to the ground. The catcher jumped to his feet and started to beat Smith on the head with the baseball! Both benches cleared and a huge fist fight broke out at home plate. Once order was instilled, and ejections made, Joe pitched a fantastic game holding the Mountaineers scoreless for 8 innings and only giving up 1 run in the 9th inning for a 3-1 win. Lefty Willis took the evening game and won that 5-3 for the sweep.

It was that time of the year when teams had to reduce their rosters to 15 men and Elmer Yoter released Hubie Fitzgerald, Cy Turner, and Hoot Gibson. Jake Plummer had also been traded to Buffalo in the International League for $1,500. It was reported that he was personally making over $100 more a month with Buffalo.

Joe got his next start against Reading on the 24th of May at home against Red Parkes. Joe gave up 2 runs in the top of the 1st inning and then held the Red Sox scoreless for the rest of the game. The game was won in the 6th inning when Elmer Yoter came to the plate with Joe on 1st base. Elmer hit a triple bringing Joe home to tie the game 2-2. He then gave Frankie Parenti the squeeze play signal as he came up to bat. Frankie laid down a nice bunt up the 3rd base line which Elmer scampered over and came home for the go ahead 3-2 winning run and Frankie made it safe to 1st base.

Heading up to Binghamton for the season's first night game Joe got the start and held the Triplets to 5 hits and 6 strikeouts in a 4-3 win. It was Joe's 3rd straight victory.

The Barons traveled to Harrisburg on the 1st of June and Joe took the mound against Dick Montague. The Senators got 11 hits off of Joe in a closely played game. The Barons offense was also quiet after getting caught in 4 double plays. It all added up to a 5-2 loss for Joe and Wilkes-Barre.

It was a battle for 1st place when the Barons traveled to Reading on the 3rd for a double header. A record 3,207 fans came out to Lauer Park to see if their Red Sox could bump the Barons out of 1st place. Joe Jackym got the start and the game turned into a hit festival and was an 8-8 tie after only 4 innings. Joe Jackym gave up the mound to Joe Semler with 1 out in the 5th inning and after 6 innings of play it was a 10-10 tie. The Barons made it 11-10 in the top of the 8th inning but the Red Sox answered with 2 runs in the bottom of the 8th inning to make it 12-11 and secured the win. Lefty Willis took the second game and lost it 4-1 and the Barons were swept and fell out of 1st place.

And things just went downhill from there. The Barons were on a serious slump losing 9 games in a row and had dropped from 1st place to 6th place by the 8th of June when they hosted Elmira. Desperately looking for a win Joe got the start against Lefty Estrada. But the Red Wings jumped out to a 1-0 lead in the top of the 1st inning and set their momentum. The game went back and forth but Wilkes-Barre lost it 5-3 and dropped down to 7th place.

Trying to shake their losing streak jinx the Barons hosted the Grays for a double header on the 10th in front of 3,000 fans. Al Reitz got the start in the early game but got hammered for a 10-4 loss. Joe took the second game and faced 3 different Williamsport pitchers in a short 5 inning game that was eventually called for rain. Down 8-1 after 4 innings the Grays sensed the game may be called due to rain. Because they were way behind they tried to stall getting the 5th inning completed so the game wouldn't count. They didn't even place a batter in the batter's box after the umpire called play ball so Joe started to pitch to an empty batter's box. That quickly got the Grays attention and got them playing. Joe was able to get the 5th inning in while it poured down rain and won it 8-1 before it was called.

But after losing the last 13 out of 15 games and falling into last place the fans were irate and letters to the sports writers were getting a lot of attention in the papers. Elmer Yoter did the usual sacking of players and signing of new talent. Those that got the cut were Joe Jackym, Gary Hannahoe their back up 1st baseman, and Joe Klinger a catcher. The new talent brought aboard were Joe Kiefer a veteran pitcher, Jimmy Horn an outfielder, Link Wasem a catcher, and Neilson Andrews a pitcher from Fordham University. The articles said that the only pitcher Yoter could depend on was Joe Semler!

Traveling to Hazelton on the 14th for a double header 1,600 fans were in Buhler Stadium to see the Thursday afternoon festivities. Joe took the early game against Johnny "Lefty" Kerdock but after giving up 5 runs in the top of the 1st inning Kerdock was replaced with Matt Wydallis. With a 5 run lead Joe cruised along to a 19-8 win. Lefty Willis got the start for the Barons in the second game and won that one 11-4. Sweeping the Mountaineers moved the Barons up to 7th place.

It was up to Elmira and a double header with the Red Wings on the 20th of June. Joe took the mound in the early game and won it 10-3. Al Reitz got the night cap duties and won that one 3-0 to get the sweep. The league was pretty bunched up in the standings and the Yotermen were only 4-1/2 games away from the 1st place leaders.

I used the term "Yotermen" which was frequently used in the papers to describe the Barons. Using the manager's name along with "men" was actually a common term used to describe a team in these days. They also really liked to refer to games as "tilts," pitchers as "twirlers," and the baseball as a "pill."

Hosting the Senators on the 21st at Artillery Park about 1,200 fans came out to see their 4th place Barons gain some more ground on the league leaders. Lefty Willis took the early game and won it 6-2. Joe Kiefer, the new addition to the Baron pitching staff took the mound in the 7 inning night cap. The Barons were up 2-0 going into the 5th inning and the Senators started to get to Kiefer so Al Reitz came in relief. By the time the 6th inning was over the Barons had a 7-6 lead. Joe Semler came in relief at the beginning of the 7th inning to secure the win. But the Senators beat him up for 2 runs to win it 8-7 and hand Joe a tough loss.

Traveling to Binghamton on the 25th the Yotermen took on the 1st place Triplets who needed a win to secure their lock on the first half championship. Joe took the mound for the Barons and his team had a 3-0 lead by the end of the 2nd inning. The Triplets got a run in the bottom of the 3rd inning to make it 3-1 and Joe held them scoreless for the next 5 innings while his teammates scored 2 more runs to make it 5-1. Binghamton was in first place for a reason and they rallied in the bottom of the 9th inning and scored 3 more runs. But it wasn't enough and Joe got the 5-4 win along with 7 strikeouts. The win also placed the Barons in 3rd place.

Joe took the mound against Charlie Eckert on the 29th at Island Park against the Senators. His teammates once again got him out to a nice 3-0 lead after the 3rd inning. But the Senators worked on Joe getting a run in the 5th inning and 2 runs in the 8th inning to tie the game at 3-3. The Senators relieved Eckert with Buddy Lake in the 8th inning and Joe kept on going for the Barons. The game went into extra innings and in the bottom of the 11th inning Harrisburg's Johnny Tyler hit a solo homer to end it 4-3.

On the road against Scranton on the 2nd of July Al Reitz got the start. He took it into the 8th inning when down 4-1 Neilson Andrews came in to relieve him to finish out the inning. The

Barons scored 4 runs in the top of the 9th inning to give them a 5-4 lead. Andrews started the 9th inning and with 1 out gave up a run to tie the game 5-5. Joe came in relief and got the Barons out of the inning and the game went into extra innings. In the top of the 11th inning the Barons scored 2 runs to take a 7-5 lead. Joe held the Miners scoreless in the bottom of the 11th to seal the win. This was also Booster Day at Brooks Field and Joe won a shirt for the second longest hit in the pregame festivities.

The first half of the league season was over and the Binghamton Triplets won the pennant with a record of 42-27. Wilkes-Barre came in 4th place with a record of 34-35. Charlie "Lefty" Willis had a record of 8-5, Joe Semler 8-7, Roger Hanlon 2-2, Al Reitz 7-8, and Joe Kiefer 3-7. Earl Johnson had been out for several weeks with an illness.

Getting his first start of the second half of the season Joe took the mound against Scranton on the 5th of July. The Yotermen got Joe out to a 13-0 lead after 8 innings. Joe did his part by holding the Miners scoreless until they finally got 3 runs in the top of the 9th inning. And with a 13-3 win it was a great way to start things off.

The Barons got their first shutout since the 8th of May when Joe pitched one at Artillery Park against Elmira on the 9th of July. *"The usually calm and easy going Pittsburgh boy put plenty of hustle into his act, hardly giving the Red Wings time to get into the box before delivering the pill."*[37] He pitched a great game retiring the side in 5 innings, only allowed 4 hits, and shutout the Red Wings 3-0.

On the road in Williamsport Joe took the mound against Luther "Bud" Thomas. The Barons jumped out to a 1 run lead in the 2nd inning and made it 2-0 in the top of the 5th inning. But the Grays answered back in the bottom of the inning to tie it up 2-2. In the top of the 8th inning the Barons made it 3-2 but the Grays once again answered back in the bottom of the inning with 4 runs to make it 6-3. The Barons scored 2 more in the top of the 9th inning but it wasn't enough and Williamsport took a 6-5 win. The loss put the Barons in a three way tie for 3rd place.

The Barons brought in a new pitcher, Lester "Lefty" Jenkins and in order to make room for him they released Neilson Andrews. Roger Hanlon who had been nursing a sore back was also released and picked up by Reading. Earl Johnson had made it back from an extended illness but was now fighting a sore wrist and tonsillitis. Elmer Yoter had also been out for a while with sore ribs and this last game with Williamsport had been his first game back. He still wasn't 100% and was playing with his ribs wrapped.

In front of 900 hometown fans Joe took the mound on the 17th against 1st place Williamsport. He had no problem coasting to a win after his teammates got him out to a 12-1 lead after the 2nd inning. It ended in a 13-3 win for Joe and placed the Barons in 4th place with a record of 7-7.

Joe won two games in a row in a sort of modified "Iron Man" feat on the 21st when the Barons took on the Mountaineers in a double header. In front of 2,000 fans Joe took the mound in the opener and went all 9 innings only allowing 4 hits. He held the mountaineers scoreless except for the 4th inning when he gave up 2 runs in a 4-2 win. Lefty Jenkins started the 7 inning nightcap and was ahead 6-4 when Joe relieved him in the 5th inning. Hazleton got 2 runs off of Joe in the top of the 7th to tie it at 6-6 and send the game into extra innings. Then the Barons answered with a run in the bottom of the 9th inning to win it 7-6. The Barons were now 11-10 and in 3rd place.

When you're on a roll keep it rolling and Joe took his winning momentum up to Binghamton on the 25th to take on the Triplets. Facing Bob Miller the game came down to the 10th inning when both teams entered it tied 3-3 and Floyd Olds came in for Miller. The Barons scored 4 runs in the top of the 10th inning and Joe held the Triplets to 3 runs in the bottom of the inning to take a 7-6 win. Bob Miller had 11 strikeouts in 9 innings and Joe threw 5 in 10 innings. It was Joe's 3rd straight win and he also moved Wilkes-Barre to 2nd place.

Hosting the Harrisburg Senators in a three game series over the 28th and 29th the Barons swept them in 3 games and inched into 1st place. Al Reitz got the start on the 28th and pitched a 4-0 shutout. Lester "Lefty" Jenkins took the mound in the early game on the 29th and won 5-2. Joe got his 4th consecutive win in the nightcap with a 3-0 shutout only allowing 5 hits. Over 4,000 fans came out to see the double header on the 29th and they got their money's worth.

Traveling to Reading to take on the Red Sox on the 1st of August Joe got the start against Roger Hanlon who had just been released by the Barons. Joe pitched a nice game striking out 6 and getting 3 of those in a row. But Hanlon also pitched a nice game and had a little more bat support beating Joe 5-1.

The papers were head lining him as "Pittsburgh Joe" when Joe Semler threw a 6-0 shutout against Elmira on the 7th of August in front of a crowd of 1,000 fans who came out to see the Barons and Red Wings complete a double header. Joe took the mound in the early game and held the visitors to 4 hits and struck out 4 to get his 16th win of the season. Lefty Jenkins took the 7 inning nightcap but half way through the 6th inning he had men on base, only 1 out, and the game tied 4-4. Elmer Yoter looked to the bull pen and Joe came out in relief. He almost got out of the inning but a run scored to make it 5-4. Joe held them scoreless in the top of the 7th but the Baron bats couldn't answer the call and the game was lost 5-4.

In front of 4,500 Williamsport fans at Bowman Park on the 13th Joe took the mound in a crucial game to maintain 1st place in the league standings. The Grays were in second but just barely and a win would push them ahead of the Barons. Joe was on his game and pitched 9 innings of scoreless baseball getting a 7-0 win.

By the 19th the Barons had fallen to 2nd place behind Scranton. Joe got the start at Artillery Park in front of 3,200 fans hosting Williamsport. He was facing off against George Miner who was also a veteran pitcher and the two of them pitched a pretty tight ball game. It all came down to the Barons pushing over one more run than the Grays in a 4-3 win.

Heading up to Elmira to play a double header the Yotermen were looking to gain some ground on the league leading Miners. Instead, they dropped both games and came out in 4th place in the league standings. Joe got the call for the early game against Art Judd and they both pitched a great game. But there was no Baron bat support and Joe lost it 1-0. Lefty Willis started the night cap and it was the same thing – no bat support – and the Barons lost 2-0.

It was another tough loss for Joe when the Barons traveled to Binghamton on the 25th of August for a double header. Robert Cooney got the start in the opener but was relieved in the 8th inning for a pinch hitter and Lefty Jenkins came in relief with a 3-2 lead. He only pitched an inning after letting the Triplets grab a 5-3 lead. The Barons tied it at 5-5 in the top of the 9th inning and Joe was brought in to pitch the bottom of the inning. He gave up the winning run for a 6-5 loss. Lefty Jenkins pitched the night cap and won it 2-1.

Joe's luck changed on the 28th when the Barons hosted the Senators in a must win game to stay in the playoff hunt. Joe went up against Lefty Klarman and Joe did about all he could do to secure a win. Pitching a nice tight game he also had 2 hits and drove in a run to get the 5-3 victory. The Barons were in 3rd place and with the season ending on the 9th of September every game counted.

The last thing the Barons needed was to get swept in a double header. And unfortunately, that's exactly what happened on the 1st of September when they hosted the Red Sox. Lefty Jenkins lost the opener 7-3 and Joe dropped the night cap 2-1. It dropped the Barons into 4th place and out of the running to make the playoffs.

Joe pitched a major milestone in baseball when he won his 20th game of the season on the 5th of September. Going against Fred Browning and the Red Sox in Reading Joe went 11 innings to secure a 3-1 win. He allowed the only run in the 3rd inning and held the Reading boys scoreless for the remaining 8 innings.

The season ended on the 9th with the Barons ending up in 5th place with a record of 32-32. The Williamsport Grays won the 2nd half pennant with a record of 41-27. They went on to play the 1st half winners the Binghamton Triplets in a 7 game championship series. The Grays won the 1934 pennant after defeating the Triplets in game 6.

Joe finished the year with the best pitching record on the Barons squad with a record of 20-12. Lester "Lefty" Jenkins was 6-4, Al Parkes 7-6, Charlie "Lefty" Willis 14-16, Al Reitz 12-15, Robert Cooney 8-11, and Earl Johnson 5-7. His 20 wins was only matched by two other pitchers in the league. Kemp Wicker of Binghamton was 20-9 and Buddy Hearn of Williamsport was 21-8. Joe was in good company because Wicker went on to play for the New York Yankees and Hearn previously pitched for the Boston Braves.

It was also reported, but not confirmed, that Joe had set a minor league record of pitching 29 complete games in a row without being relieved, from May 7th to September 1st. And if you read over his game summaries it is very unusual for Joe to be relieved, and if he starts a game he usually finished it.[38]

Joe usually got involved in some sort of post season game in the Pittsburgh area and this year he was selected to play with the Deans traveling exhibition team. The team was made up of Jay "Dizzy" Dean and his brother Paul "Daffy" Dean along with players they picked up in whatever city they played in. The Dean Brothers were major league pitchers and had just won the World Series with the St. Louis Cardinals in the first week of October. They drew in huge crowds and in the two weeks since the World Series had made over $20,000. Dizzy was said to have made $3,000 alone last week in Cleveland with the exhibition show.

Local manager Billy Fuchs had put together a group of minor and major league players to play with the Deans. Like Joe these players had finished up their minor and major league seasons and had returned home to their families in the Pittsburgh area. The team consisted of minor league players Joe Semler, Ollie Carnegie, Dick Goldberg, Hal King, Elmer Trapp, and major leaguers Julius "Moose" Solters of the Boston Red Sox, and Bill Swift of the Pittsburgh Pirates to name a few. They would be playing the local Negro players consisting mainly of the Pittsburgh Crawford's called the All-Stars. Players like Satchel Paige, Josh Gibson, Vic Harris,

Judy Johnson and others known for playing with the Crawford's and Homestead Grays.

The game was played on the 23rd of October at Forbes Field and Satchel Paige took the mound for the All-Stars and Dizzy Dean for the Deans. The Deans were winning 2-0 after 2 innings when Harry Kincannon came in for Paige and Joe Semler for the Deans. In the bottom of the 5th inning the Deans were ahead 3-1 when the All-Stars Vic Harris came to bat with 2 outs. He hit a light rap that rolled just ahead of home plate and started to run to 1st base. The catcher picked up the ball and wildly threw it to 1st and it got by the 1st baseman. Harris rounded 1st and made it to 2nd base. Dizzy Dean motioned to the home plate umpire that Harris had interfered with the throw to 1st base by running outside of the baseline. The umpire agreed and called Harris out. Harris stormed in from 2nd base and started to beat up the umpire which cleared both benches and a fistfight broke out at home plate. Even the fans jumped onto the field and into the melee. The police finally broke it up and Harris was ejected from the game. The All-Stars tied it up in the bottom of the 8th inning when Josh Gibson hit a 2 run homer to tie the game and Curt Harris drove in the winning run winning it 4-3.

About 43 years later my dad asked Joe about playing in this game and he remembered it in detail. He said it was really tough pitching teams like that when every player was so good. He vividly remembered giving up that 2 run homer in the bottom of the 8th inning and said even though he lost, he felt he pitched a good game against such great talent.[47]

Nashville Volunteers 1935

It was headline news in January that Joe had been traded by the Barons to the Nashville Volunteers in the Southern Association League for four players. The players were Al Joyner a 1st baseman, Paul O'Malley a catcher, Bob Dueker an outfielder, and Harlan McClelland a pitcher. The deal also gave Nashville the rights to recall any two of the players if they needed them. A benefit of the deal for the Barons was that by having this player recall arrangement the Barons were now loosely affiliated with the New York Giants major league organization.

But Joe wasn't happy with the deal and had notified Nashville that he wasn't going to accept the terms of the contract and sent it back unsigned. The sticking point seemed to be the fact that he wasn't going to be paid any more in Nashville than what he was making at Wilkes-Barre. And Joe wanted a pay raise if he was going to leave and said Nashville needed to increase their salary offer. The Southern Association was a Class-A league just like the New York-Pennsylvania League but were considered to be a higher caliber league than the NYP. So, I can see why Joe was wanting more money to play with them.

The reason the Southern league was considered a higher caliber of Class-A baseball was that they in fact had a higher caliber of player, played in larger cities, and in front of larger crowds. Back in the NYP League crowds ranged up to 4,000. In the Southern league it was up to 12,000.

Joe eventually came to terms with Nashville and told them that he would report as soon as he finished building a house that he was committed to complete with his father in their construction business. The Nashville papers said that his initial contract was the same one that he eventually signed so he wasn't getting a pay increase. I'm not sure why he initially baulked, unless he was just trying to call their bluff on a pay raise.

Joe joined the team at their spring training facility in Tallahassee, Florida on the 21st of March and was one of the last two players to arrive. The picture on the following page is Joe at their spring training facility at Centennial Field in Tallahassee, Florida.

It was reported in a Nashville paper that *"He's baldheaded and looks like he's about 45. And don't think he doesn't know plenty about pitching. You have to in order to win twenty games in that loop."*[39] Although Joe was 35 years old the Nashville newspapers were fixated on the fact that he was actually in his early 20's and just looked old for his age.

Joe Semler at spring training in Tallahassee, Florida

Zach Smith who played with Joe at Wilkes-Barre last year, and now with Nashville, is quoted in the papers describing his pitching style as an *"orthodox type of hurler, with a good curve and a better fast ball. He employs the latter more often and sometimes throws sidearm. Too, he is experimenting with a knuckler to add to his repertoire"*[40]

During spring training Nashville played the other teams in the Southern Association in exhibition games consisting of the Atlanta Crackers, Birmingham Barons, Chattanooga Lookouts, Knoxville Smokies, Little Rock Travelers, Memphis Chickasaws, Nashville Volunteers, and New Orleans Pelicans. They also had training twice a day in the morning and afternoon.

The team had to cut their roster from around 30 players down to 20 towards the end of March. Most of these were pitchers vying for the 6 open slots. The picture below shows the five pitchers that were reported to have tentatively made the team and there were 6 other pitchers competing for that last sixth slot. Pictured below are; Byron Speece, Tiny Chaplin, Hal Stafford, Sharkey Eiland, and Joe Semler.

1935 Nashville Pitchers as of late March[41]

The team finished up in Florida on the 31st and traveled back to Nashville on the 1st of April. They needed to get back to Nashville to take on the major league Washington Senators in an exhibition game on the 2nd of April.

The sports writers reporting on Joe in early April are skeptical as to whether or not he can handle the Southern hitters and that he really hasn't gotten into shape since he had arrived a few weeks ago in Florida. But then again he hasn't been put in a situation to demonstrate his pitching ability and only given an inning here and there in exhibition.

Joe was scheduled to get the start against the major league Cleveland Indians and New York Yankees in early April but the games were rained out. Finally, he got a start on the 10th of April against Central State, a team from the local Central State Hospital. He went 3 innings, struck out 2, and held Central State scoreless before being relieved. He was also credited with the 6-1 win.

Nashville needed to get down to 6 pitchers by the 15th and Joe's job was in jeopardy. He was battling it out for that last position with a pitcher named Linville "Lyn" Watkins. The papers were saying that Watkins looked like a better option because he was in his early 20's compared to Joe being in his mid-30's and that Nashville owned Watkins and Joe was on a pricy contract.

But opening day came on the 16th and Joe and Lyn were still on the team when the official roster was submitted to the league and they were carrying 7 pitchers on their roster. Nashville played their opener at Chattanooga in front of a crowd of over 8,800 and Sharkey Eiland got the start. He pitched a nice game and it was tied 5-5 after 9 innings. In the top of the 10th inning Nashville scored a run to make it 6-5. Joe was brought in relief in the bottom of the 10th and he stuck out the first batter he faced with three curve balls. The next batter singled and he walked the next 2 to load the bases. He then got the next two batters to weakly pop out and Nashville won 6-5. Some papers were reporting that Joe had gotten the win but officially Eiland deservedly got it.

After the game Chattanooga protested the pitching classification of Joe. Nashville was considering Joe as a Class-B player when in fact he was a Class-A player. Southern Association rules stated that a team had to have a certain amount of Class-A, Class –B, and rookies on their team, even though the league was classified as Class-A. Chattanooga's gripe was that Nashville was playing with too many Class-A players.

To avoid forfeiting the game that they had won with Joe pitching Nashville immediately notified the league that they had misclassified Joe and would re-list him as Class-A from here on out. In doing so they needed to remove a Class-A player from the roster to stay within their Class-A limit. Unfortunately, the player to be released was his old Baron teammate Zach Smith who was returned to the NYP League.

It was Joe's first game and he was the center of attention!

Playing Chattanooga at home in Nashville on the 19th the Volunteers played in front of 4,600 fans at the Sulphur Dell, their ball park. Byron Speece got the start and midway through the 4th inning, and behind 7-2, Joe came in relief. Joe pitched two scoreless innings and then got taken for a solo homer in the 7th to make it 8-2. Hal Stafford relieved Joe and pitched the last 2 innings in an 8-2 Nashville loss.

Lyn Watkins got the start against Chattanooga at home on the 21st. It was actually a close game and was tied 1-1 going into the top of the 9th inning. Then Lyn got banged up for 2 runs to make it 3-1 in favor of Chattanooga. Joe came in relief with 2 outs already recorded and got the last one without incident to end the inning. The Volunteers couldn't answer in the bottom of the 9th and lost 3-1.

Joe was actually doing really well at this early point in the season and he was the second best pitcher on the roster behind Eiland who had the teams only win. Nashville as a team wasn't doing all that well and was in 6th place out of 8 teams with a record of 2-4.

Joe finally got his chance to start on the 24th against 1st place Memphis. Playing in Memphis at Russwood Park Joe went 3 innings before coming out of the game with a sore arm. He was down 3-1 and Hal Stafford came in relief. The Volunteers came back in the top of the 5th inning scoring 3 runs to make it 4-3. But the Chickasaws came back in the bottom of the 9th inning scoring 2 runs to win the game 5-4.

Joe got his next start against the Birmingham Barons at the Sulphur Dell in Nashville on the 1st of May. His arm was just fine and Joe had his curve and fastball working well as he held the Barons scoreless for the first 8 innings facing only 27 batters. But in the 9th inning his teammates had 2 fielding errors which cost him the game. With 1 out an infield hit that should have gone for a double play was boggled. Then an easy throw to 1st base went wild. In the end Joe lost 4-2.

At this point in the season Joe was gaining respect with the sports writers and they deemed him the fastest working pitcher on the Nashville team. They said his curve and fast ball weren't the best, but he had great control, cuts the plate corners, and doesn't get into many jams. And on the 6th of May Nashville thought Joe was good enough to make a permanent member of the team, ending his contract probationary period.

Back on the mound Joe was pitching at Rickwood Field in Birmingham, Alabama against the Barons on the 8th. He gave up a 3 run homer to the Barons right fielder Nick Etten in the 1st inning and another solo homer to him in the 3rd inning. That about sealed the loss for Joe in a 6-1 Baron victory. Joe was now 0-2 and Nashville 11-10 and in 4th place.

Traveling to New Orleans on the 11th Joe was getting a grand ole tour of the south. Playing at Heinemann Park Sharkey Eiland got the start. But after working 2/3's of an inning and giving up 4 runs Hal Stafford relieved him and finally got out of the 1st inning. Stafford gave up 3 runs in the 3rd inning and after getting weak in the 5th inning Joe came in. Down 7-1 Joe took it the rest of the way giving up a run in the 5th inning and 3 runs in the 7th inning for an 11-1 loss.

Tragedy struck Joe as he was preparing to take the mound on the 18th against Atlanta at the Sulphur Dell. He received word that his wife Cyrilla had passed away suddenly back in Pittsburgh. He immediately left for home taking the noon train. Cyrilla had been suffering from gallstones for about four months and unexpected died at home of a pulmonary embolism. Her death was tragic in so many ways. Joe hadn't seen her since he left for spring training in Florida in late March. He also had 4 young children at home who were now without their mother.

The tragedy ended Joe's time with Nashville and he was initially put on the suspended list to make room for another player on the roster. He finished up playing in 7 games, with a record of 0-2, pitched 29-1/3 innings, and struck out 12. He had 9 at bats and was hitless.

Towards the end of May Joe asked for his release from Nashville and he was assigned back to Wilkes-Barre who were still under the watchful eye of Elmer Yoter. But there were problems back in Wilkes-Barre. The Barons as a baseball team were actually doing fantastic and were 17-8 and in 1st place. The Barons as an organization was in financial trouble and the owners were saying that if attendance didn't pick up they were going to sell the team. Management was entertaining offers from cities in New York and said they couldn't understand the low turnout since the Barons were in first place. It was a bit strange because Wilkes-Barre had always had a big fan base that provided big crowds at the games. But it was the Depression and times were tough.

Joe Semler with Nashville[42]

Wilkes-Barre Barons
1935 to 1936

Back with Wilkes-Barre Joe reported the 30th of May and took the mound against the Senators in Harrisburg. In front of a crowd of 1,000 Joe picked up right where he left off in the NYP League and beat the Senators. The game was tied 5-5 in the top of the 9th inning when Joe doubled to center and then took 3rd base on a wild throw. He scored off of a single by Hubie Fitzgerald to take the lead 6-5. Going into the bottom of the 9th inning he pitched to one batter and then his old buddy Earl Johnson came in relief to finish the game up. Joe got the win and it kept the Barons in 1st place by a half a game with a record of 20-9. I know that after the tragic loss of Cyrilla it must have been good for Joe to be back around his Baron teammates.

Joe Semler with Wilkes-Barre Barons circa 1935

The Barons were hosting Elmira on the 4th of June in what was supposed to be a double header. But rain cancelled the early game so they just got in one 9 inning contest in front of a small rain shy crowd. It's interesting that they describe the grounds crew using oil heaters to dry the field out and for the slippery spots they used sand. With the field ready Joe took the mound and was on a roll. While the Barons offensively racked up 5 runs Joe held the Pioneers (yes they changed their name once again) scoreless for 7 innings. Finally in the 8th inning they got Joe for a run but it wasn't enough to catch the Barons and Joe won it 5-1. He rounded out the game with a hit, drove in 2 runs, and struck out 4. It was in the 4th inning when he drove in the 2 runs on a single. But he tried to stretch it into a double and was tagged out at 2nd base.

Hosting the Triplets in a double header at Artillery Park on the 7th the Barons sent Joe to the mound in the opener. He got hit for 4 runs in the 1st inning and never made it out of the inning before being relieved by Julian Wesco. He took it to the 9th inning before being relieved by Jim "Lefty" McCloskey who retired the Triplets in order. But the final was 5-2 and Joe got the loss. Jack Kimball got the start in the night cap and lost it 7-5. The double loss dropped the Barons into 2nd place behind Scranton.

It's reported that Joe had a sore arm in yesterday's game with the Triplets and that he had been nursing it since his return against the Senators on the 30th of May. Apparently he has rheumatism in his pitching arm and can't pitch. Elmer Yoter placed him on the suspended list for 10 days and signed Johnny

Krider to replace Joe. It's also reported that while recovering Joe had a bunch of his teeth pulled on the advice of his physician. Joe used tobacco pretty heavily and had a sweet tooth to boot so he more than likely had periodontal disease, which can contribute to health issues. That's probably why he had so many teeth removed at the relatively young age of 35. That's just my opinion since I never came across any mention of a baseball type of injury like a ball, bat, or arm to his face that would have caused a dental problem.

It's pretty amazing that Joe hadn't had more problems with his pitching arm since he had been throwing for 15 years now with relatively few issues. I really don't think he worked out in the off season, besides swinging a hammer as a carpenter. As a matter of fact the Nashville papers were reporting that the reason he was taking so long to get in shape when he arrived at spring training was that he hadn't touched a baseball the previous 4 months over the winter. And that sort of makes sense for that era of being an athlete. Joe was too busy working over the off season and probably not concerned with a baseball workout. Maybe he just looked at the offseason as a time to totally rest his arm and he would get it in shape during spring training.

Joe made his return on the 22nd in a double header against Williamsport at Artillery Park. Johnny Krider got the start in the early game and lost it 3-0. Joe got the 7 inning night cap and won it 6-5. The win put the Barons only a game behind 1st place Scranton. With the 1st half of the season ending on the 30th of June, only a week away, every game was critical.

The Barons were in 1st place on the 26th when they traveled to Reading to take on the Brooks at Lauer's Park. Reading was previously in the Red Sox major league farm system but this year is in the Brooklyn Dodger farm system, hence the name change. Joe got the start against Charley Eckert and he was ahead 2-1 after 5 innings and then it all went south. He gave up 3 runs in the 6th inning, 4 runs in the 7th inning, and 2 runs in the 8th inning for a 10-3 loss. The loss didn't knock the Barons out of 1st place but they were just a fraction of a game ahead of Scranton.

The Barons were in 2nd place going into Saturday the 29th and had the perfect chance to move into 1st place when Scranton came to Wilkes-Barre for a double header. Charlie Willis got the start for the early game and won 5-1 which put the Barons only a game behind Scranton. Joe got the start in the night cap and was head 2-1 after 1-2/3 innings but had to come out because his arm was giving him problems again. Calvin "Johnny" Lowe, a newly obtained pitcher, came in and held it at 3-3 going into the 9th inning. He came out in the 9th inning and Charlie Willis came in to close it. But the Miners got him for 3 runs and he lost it 6-3. That put the Barons 2 games behind Scranton.

The next day the two teams took it up again for another double header in Scranton. This was it. If the Barons could win two games off of Scranton today they would tie them as 1st half champions. Scranton fans knew how important these games were and 11,000 fans, the second largest crowd in history, came out to watch. John Krider got the start and it was a close game with the Barons leading 3-2 going into the bottom of the 9th inning when Calvin Lowe came in. He gave away the tying run and the game went into extra innings. Earl Johnson came in to take it after Lowe and he gave away the winning run in the bottom of the 11th inning for a 4-3 loss.

That was it for the 1st half of the leagues season and Scranton had won the 1st half championship. The two teams tried to play the second game of the double header but they couldn't get the jubilant fans off the field from the first game win and the second game was cancelled.

After the series with Scranton Joe packed his bags and headed back home to McKees Rocks to rest his arm. And the Wilkes-Barre owners who were complaining since the beginning of the season that they may have to sell the team seem to be at least breaking even because they stayed for the 2nd half of the season. Reading on the other hand called it quits and the team was moved to Allentown under new management. They were now the Allentown Brooks.

After almost two weeks of rest Joe wired Elmer Yoter on the 6th of July that he would be rejoining the team on Friday the 12th while they were on the road in Williamsport. It's a good thing the Yotermen were on the road because the Susquehanna River had spilled over its banks and Artillery field was under a foot of water. If the river hadn't receded and dried out by next Tuesday when the Barons returned home they planned on playing at Wyoming Stadium in Kingston.

Joe wasn't doing that bad so far this year and had a 3-2 record with the Barons. And that's with an arm that was giving him trouble. He met the Barons in Williamsport and suited up for the start on the 13th of July. The Barons were just behind the 1st place Grays in the standings. Joe pitched 6 innings and was winning 4-3 before being relieved by John Krider. He had given up the lead in the 7th inning but regained it in the top of the 9th inning 6-5. He came out and was relieved by Julian Wesco in the bottom of the 9th inning. But Wesco was wild and immediately replaced by Earl Johnson who kept the 6-5 win. Krider got credit for the victory which put the Barons in 1st place. The following day the Barons swept the Grays in a double header and they moved 3 games ahead of Williamsport.

Hazleton traveled to Wilkes-Barre for a double header on the 16th and Johnny Krider got the start in the early game. He was ahead 8-2 going into the 5th inning when he started to get hit hard and gave up 3 runs with 2 outs. Joe came in relief and got out of the inning without any harm. He took the game to the end for an 11-6 win. Julian Wesco started the night cap and lost it 6-1.

The new team from Allentown came to Wilkes-Barre on the 20th and Joe went up against Harvey Green who later in the year went on to pitch in the major leagues for the Brooklyn Dodgers. But today was all Joe as he shutout the Brooks in a 3-0 win.

It was father and son day at Artillery Park and the pair got in for the price of one for a double header against Harrisburg on the 24th. About 1,200 fans were in attendance to see Joe take the mound in the first game. He won it 4-1 and the only run he gave up came off of a solo homer by his old teammate Jake Plummer. Johnny "Lefty" Kerdock who was just brought aboard from Hazleton started the night cap and made a good impression winning it 2-1. The sweep gave the Barons their 8th straight win and a nice lead in 1st place.

The Triplets usually give Joe trouble and it was no different on the 28th when he started against them in the first game of a double header at Johnson Park. The first batter Joe faced hit a leadoff homer to make it 1-0. He gave up 5 more runs in the 2nd inning to make it 6-0 and was sent to the showers and "Lefty" Kerdock came in. He gave up 5 runs in the 3rd inning to make it 11-0. He calmed down after that and held Binghamton scoreless for the remainder of the game for an 11-1 Baron loss. Charlie Willis started the night cap and fared much better with a 6-1 win.

Travelling to Allentown to take on the Brooks at Fairgrounds Field on the 30th Joe got the start against "Dutch" Bergman. Joe was out to a nice 6-0 lead after 2 innings. It was 6-1 going into the 7th inning when Joe started to get hit and gave up 3 runs, had two men on base, and only one out. That was it for Joe and Johnny Krider came in and let the 2 men on base score to tie it 6-6 before getting out of the inning. It stayed tied and after 11 innings the game was called due to darkness.

On the road in Harrisburg the league leading Barons should have had no problem with the 6th place Senators on the 3rd of

August. Joe took the mound against Buddy Lake. The 1st inning went scoreless and in the bottom of the 2nd inning Joe was taken for 7 runs. So, after only 1-2/3 innings of work Earl Johnson came in relief. Before it was over the Senators got 3 runs off of him while Buddy Lake pitched a shutout 10-0 win. The loss was one of several over the past couple of days and the Barons 1st place lead had been cut down to 2 games ahead of Scranton and Hazleton.

The Barons came off a dismal road trip and took on Scranton in front of 800 fans on the 6th. It was father and son day again and "Lefty" Kerdock got the start. But he only lasted 1-1/3 innings before giving up 3 runs in the 2nd inning and letting the Miners take a 4-3 lead. Joe came in relief with 1 out and gave up another run before getting out of the inning. He gave up another run in the 7th inning to make it 6-3. After being taken out of the game for a pinch hitter in the bottom of the 8th inning Earl Johnson came in to pitch the top of the 9th inning and gave up a run to make it 7-3. The Barons rallied in the bottom of the 9th inning scoring 2 runs but it wasn't enough and lost 7-5. The Barons were still in 1st place but just by a fraction ahead of Scranton.

Joe got another tough loss on the 8th of August when Elmira came to Wilkes-Barre for a double header. Johnny Krider got the start in the early game but after 7-2/3 innings he was down 6-5. "Lefty" Kerdock came in to finish the top of the 8th inning and gave up a run making it 7-5. In the bottom of the 8th inning the Barons tied it 7-7. Joe came in to pitch the 9th inning and gave up the winning run, a solo homer, for an 8-7 Pioneer win.

Charlie Willis got the start in the night cap and won it 2-1. It was his 20th win of the year and he was at 20-6. The Barons retained 1st place because the Miners also split a double header.

The Triplets played the Barons a visit on the 10th and Joe took the mound in front of a small crowd of 500 fans. Joe was on his game and he had plenty of Baron bat support with everyone getting a hit in the game except the right fielder Hal "Midget" Saffer. Joe had 2 hits and scored twice in the 14-1 Baron win. Scranton had won their last 5 games but the Barons were still ahead of them in the standings.

Travelling to Williamsport on the 14th Joe got the start at Bowman Park against Al Benton who was currently on loan to the Grays from the major league Philadelphia Athletics. He would go on to have a lengthy major league career. The Barons took a 3 run lead in the top of the 3rd inning when Joe bunted to Benton and he overthrew the 2nd basemen in an attempted double play. The error led to 3 Baron runs. Joe was out to a 4-2 lead going into the 7th inning and after giving up a run half way through the inning Johnny Krider came in relief. He held on to the 5-3 win for Joe. Scranton had been on a winning streak and had just nudged the Barons out of 1st place.

Joe was on a roll when the Hazleton Mountaineers came to Artillery Park on the 16th. He went 10 innings pitching a great game allowing the visitors only 4 hits up until the 8th inning when they got a run to tie the game 1-1. Finally in the 10th inning Joe singled but was put out at 2nd base. The Mountaineer pitcher, Rusty Bowers, then went on to load the bases and walk in the winning run. Joe happily took the 2-1 win. The victory edged the Baron back in 1st place.

Joe made it 4 wins in a row when the Grays were back at Artillery Park on the 20th in front of a scant 200 fans. He took the mound and it was 2-2 after 3 innings. He held the Grays scoreless after that and the Barons picked up 2 more runs in the bottom of the 6th inning to make it 4-2. The Barons were pulling out ahead in 1st place with Hazleton behind them.

Playing a double header at Fairgrounds Field in Allentown on the 24th Joe got the start in the early game. The Barons went up 3-0 in the 5th inning when Joe walked and was driven in by Hubie Fitzgerald and Hal Saffer drove in the other 2 runs. The Brooks scored once in the 6th and 7th innings but it wasn't enough and Joe got his 5th straight win. "Lefty" Kerdock got the start in the night cap and lost it 2-1. The Barons were now 2 games up on 2nd place Elmira.

I never took Joe for being a fast guy but it was Booster Day when the Barons took on Allentown on the 24th and Joe won a box of cigars in the 50 yard dash. Elmer Yoter also won a box of cigars circling the bases in 15 seconds.

On the road in Binghamton Joe got the start against the Triplets on the 27th. He was ahead 3-0 going into the 4th inning when he started to give up runs. The Triplets had pulled ahead 5-3 going into the bottom of the 7th inning when Joe gave up 3 more runs to make it 8-3. Johnny Krider came in relief and held the game for an 8-3 loss. The Barons fell to 3rd place and the Mountaineers jumped to 1st place.

Up in Elmira on the 29th Earl Johnson took the mound at Dunn Field. He was behind 3-1 going into the 8th inning when the Barons scored 3 runs in the top of the 8th inning. Joe came in and held the Pioneers scoreless in the bottom of the 8th and 9th innings to get the 4-3 win. The victory didn't help the Barons in the standings and they had drifted back to 4th place.

Traveling to Scranton for a double header on the 31st of August Charlie Willis took the mound against Joe Shaute in the early game in front of 2,500 Miner fans. He lost it 4-0 and Shaute got his 21st win of the season. Joe took the night cap and lost that one 5-1.

The next day Johnny "Lefty" Kerdock took the mound. The Miners jumped out to a 2-0 lead in the bottom of the 1st inning and went scoreless until the Barons tied it up in the top of the 8th inning 2-2. Joe came in relief and it went to the bottom of the 12th inning when a close call at the plate gave the Miners a 3-2 win. With a Miner on 2nd base Joe tried to pick him off but the ball ended up in center field. The runner tried to make it home and Hubie Fitzgerald made a great throw to home plate. But the ball took a weird bounce in front of the catcher and went over his head allowing the winning run.

A day before the Barons season ended Joe headed home to be with his four kids. It had been a year that started out so promising at Nashville. But after going 0-2 with them Cyrilla passed away and he came back to Wilkes-Barre. He pitched well with the Barons finishing the season with a 12-8 record.

Charlie Willis was 22-10, Johnny Krider 14-12, Earl Johnson 11-13, and Johnny Kerdock 8-10.

Wilkes-Barre finished the 2nd half of the season in 4th place with a record of 38-31. The 2nd half champions were the Binghamton Triplets who would go on and play the 1st half winning Scranton Miners in a 7 games series to decide the League Champion. The Triplets were eventually crowned the 1935 New York-Pennsylvania League Champions when they beat Scranton in the final 7th game of the series.

Like Joe most of the Barons went home to work in the off season. Frankie Parenti the 2nd baseman went back to Chicago and his physical instructor job. Bunny Griffith the shortstop to his government inspector job with a talking machine company in New Jersey, Johnny Kerdock did clerical work for a mine in Mount Carmel, and Charlie Willis and Earl Johnson were promised jobs with local coal mines but they didn't pan out so they returned home looking for work. Some like Hubie Fitzgerald, Johnny Krider and Joe Dwyer continued to play with exhibition teams as late into the season as they could.

1936:

As the season started to get underway Elmer Yoter is no longer with the Barons and has moved over to Scranton. Jake Pitler who managed Joe at Hazleton will be taking over at Wilkes-Barre. Harrisburg isn't fielding a team this year. And the Barons will be under new management this year and ownership is made of a group of investors.

Spring training got underway on the 20th of April at the Wyoming Seminary Field due to Artillery Field being readied for the season opener against Scranton on the 30th of April.

Joe held out until the last minute to sign and didn't show up to Wilkes-Barre until the 29th of April. As usual I'm sure he was negotiating for the best deal he could get from the Barons. I'm sure Elmer Yoter over with Scranton was also trying to get him to sign there.

It was opening day on the 30th of April at Artillery Park and after a parade the New York-Pennsylvania League president ran the flag up the flagpole and the Mayor of Wilkes-Barre threw out the first pitch. Johnny Krider got the start against Bill Gilvary but after giving up 5 runs in the 2nd inning newcomer Johnny Kohlman came in relief. He lasted until the middle of the 4th inning and was relieved by Joe Semler after giving up 7 runs. By the time Joe took the mound the Barons were behind 12-2! Joe gave up a run in the 5th and 8th innings for a 14-5 loss.

It didn't get much better the following day when the Barons travelled to Scranton. Johnny Kerdock took the mound at Crystal Gardens Stadium against Tex Nelson but after giving up 8 runs in the 5th inning Joe came in. By that time it was a 9-3 ball game and once again there was little Joe could do. He gave up 1 more run before it was over for a 10-5 loss. Elmer Yoter who was managing and playing 3rd base for Scranton had 4 hits in the game, 2 singles, a double, and a triple.

Heading back to Wilkes-Barre to play Scranton on the 2nd of May and a double header with Elmira on the 3rd the Barons set an attendance record. Over 4,600 fans paid to see the double header against Elmire. There were so many fans that the ticket booths were over run and 800 fans missed the game waiting on tickets. Johnny Krider pitched a 6-1 win over Scranton on Saturday. Charlie Willis started the opening game on Sunday but got behind 4-2 after 6 innings and Joe came in relief. He gave up 3 runs but the Barons scored 3 runs for a 7-5 loss. Johnny Kerdock handled the night cap with a 3-1 win. All the action put the Barons in 3rd place in the league standings.

Hosting the Triplets on the 6th Joe got his first start of the season. It didn't go well after giving up 5 runs in the 2nd inning and getting behind 5-1. By the 5th inning he was behind 7-2 and by the 7th inning it was 9-2. Johnny Krider came in relief and the Barons scored 4 runs in the bottom of the 8th inning. This apparently didn't go over well with the Triplets manager and two of his players who were all ejected from the game for using foul language towards the umpire. The game ended with a 10-6 Triplet win.

Heading up to Elmira for a two game series on the 9th and 10th of May Johnny Kerdock got the start in the Saturday game. He had a 5-2 lead going into the 7th inning when Joe came in relief. He held the Pioneers scoreless for the remaining 3 innings for the 5-2 win. Charlie Willis started the Sunday game and lost it 5-3. After the series the Barons announced that they had releases Johnny Kohlman and signed Bob Cooney.

Joe took the mound in Binghamton on the 12th and was facing Atley Donald. Atley would go on to play for the New York Yankees and set a major league record for the most consecutive wins by a rookie. He was also said to be the fastest pitcher at the time throwing a 98 mph fastball. It's probably why he had 6 strikeouts in the game and Joe just had 1. But Joe pitched a better game and had better bat support in a 7-4 win.

Hosting Williamsport at Artillery Park on the 15th Bob Cooney got the start. The game was tied 6-6 going into the 7th inning. Bob gave up 2 runs to make it 8-6 and with 2 men on base and 2 outs Joe came in relief. He got out of the inning and held the Grays scoreless while the Barons scored 2 runs in the bottom of the 7th inning and 1 run in the bottom of the 8th inning to win it 9-8 and give Joe his second win.

Hazleton came to Artillery Park for a double header on the 17th and 4,700 fans showed up. Joe started the early game and got behind 3-2 going into the 8th inning and Bob Cooney relieved him. He gave up a run in the top of the 9th inning and the Barons lost 4-2. Charlie Willis took the night cap and had better luck winning it 11-5. The Barons were currently in 5th place in the league standings.

The Barons shook up their pitching staff and signed Charlie Blethem from Knoxville in the Southern League and released Johnny Krider and Bob Cooney. Johnny Kerdock has been on the suspended list after crashing his bicycle into a cement wall and hurting his pitching arm.

Traveling to Williamsport on the 21st Joe took the mound against Eddie Smith. Joe didn't last long and after giving up 3 runs in the 2nd inning and 2 runs in the 3rd inning he was relieved by Matt Holmes. After he gave up 4 more runs Johnny Kerdock just off the suspended list came in. He finished up the 9th inning and the Grays won it 9-3. Eddie Smith tied a league record with 17 strikeouts in the game.

The Barons were in Allentown on the 25th of May and Joe took the mound against Harry Eisenstat. Joe had lady luck on his side and wouldn't be denied a win today. Two Brooks's runners were tagged out at home plate in the 4th inning to keep them scoreless. And even Eisenstat pitching a 2 hit game couldn't stop Joe as he cruised to a 2-0 shutout win.

Getting the start at Eagle Park on the 29th against York Joe was going against Harry Shuman, a former major league hurler. Joe got ahead 2 runs in the 1st inning and the Barons added 1 more in the 3rd inning and another run in the 5th inning. Meanwhile Joe held the White Roses scoreless through 8 innings. Finally in the bottom of the 9th inning they scored 2 runs but it wasn't enough and Joe won 4-2. Joe had 5 strikeouts, held York to 5 hits, and had a hit in the game.

Playing Elmer Yoter's Miners in Scranton Johnny Kerdock got the start in front of 3,000 spectators on the 31st. He was going against Joe Shaute. They both pitched a pretty good ball game and it was scoreless going into the bottom of the 4th inning. The Miners picked up a run in the bottom of the 4th, 5th, and 6th innings to make it 3-0. Joe came in the bottom of the 8th inning and held them scoreless in hopes of the Barons getting some runs in the top of the 9th inning. But it didn't happen and the Miners won 3-0. The Barons were in 4th place with a record of 19-17.

Back home at Artillery Park on the 2nd of June Frank Tubbs took the mound. It was only his second start this season and he had been on the suspension list for over a month due to an injury. It was a tough start for him and he was behind 5-0 after 1-2/3 innings of work. Joe came in relief and he was taken for 10 singles resulting in 6 runs in 2-2/3 innings. He was relieved by Matt Holmes who gave up 2 more runs in a 13-3 beating. After the game Johnny Kerdock was released to the Scranton Miners where Elmer Yoter was said to be happy to have him.

Taking on Elmira at Artillery Park on the 4th in front of 2,100 fans Clarence Blethem got the start. It was the second game under the lights at Artillery Park this season. The game was tied 4-4 going into the 8th inning when the leadoff batter hit a double. Fearing that Blethem was getting tired Jake Pitler sent in Joe to take over. But bad pitching and 2 errors by Murphy the shortstop let 6 runs score. The final was 10-4 in favor of the Pioneers.

Just an interesting fact about Artillery Park, Babe Ruth hit the longest home run ever recorded in baseball in it. It was in an exhibition game in 1926 and it travelled 650 feet! And no Joe didn't pitch it to him, a guy named Ernie Corkran did.

It was another tough relief experience for Joe the following day when the Barons took on Elmira at Artillery Park. Johnny Day took the mound and in the 1st inning there were 2 fielding errors, 2 stolen bases, and a walked in run that gave the Pioneers a 1-0 lead. By the 6th inning the Pioneers were up 6-3. Matt Holmes came in to handle the 7th inning and kept the visitors scoreless while the Barons scored 4 runs in the bottom of the 7th inning to take the lead 7-6. In the top of the 8th inning Holmes loaded the bases and Joe came in. He gave up two runs before getting out of the inning and it ended in a 9-7 Pioneer win.

Joe had a win slip away from him when Scranton came to Wilkes-Barre on the 8th of June. Joe took the mound against Joe Shaute and they had a nice pitching duel going on with Joe leading 5-4 heading into the 9th inning. Joe got the first batter out and the next batter hit a grounder to the 1st baseman but it took a weird hop over his head and put the tying runner on 1st base. With 2 left handed batters coming up Jake Pitler brought in Johnny Day to face them. He ended up walking them and gave up the tying run before getting out of the inning. The game was tied 5-5 going into the 11th inning when Day gave up 3 runs in the top of the 11th to lose the game 8-5.

After the game Joe was surprisingly released by the Barons. Usually when a player is released it doesn't make big headlines, just a note in the sport columns, but this certainly made headlines in the Wilkes-Barre papers. I think the reason that everyone was surprised was because Joe wasn't pitching that badly and had a 4-3 record at the time. And he wasn't being used by Jake Pitler as a starter which he was better suited, but more as relief pitcher. Joe is quoted in the local paper as not being that upset about his release and said *"The building boom is spreading out home and my father needs me, but I love baseball."*[45] He told the paper that he was going to head home for a few days and think over his options.

Back in McKees Rocks Joe was offered a job with Scranton, Elmira, Williamsport and even Nashville but he turned them down. Instead he signed with his old team Dormont in the City League under the management of Bill Fuchs. There was more to staying than just the family business. Joe had met Grace Gunsallus and they had just gotten married. So I'm sure he wanted to stay close to his 4 children and new wife.

He got his first start with them on the 1st of July against the Crafton Stars at home in Dormont. It wasn't an official City League game but rather an exhibition game in between the 1st and 2nd half of the season. Taking the mound against Herb Hurst Joe was up 3-0 but the lead quickly disappeared and he lost the game 11-5.

The Barons realizing that they probably cut Joe to quickly were trying to talk him back into re-joining the team but he declined the offer. The Barons ended up coming in next to last place in the 1st half of the season. Elmer Yoter and Scranton won the 1st half of the season championship and I'm sure he was also trying to get Joe to join them.

Playing the Homestead Grays at Dormont on the 6th of July in another exhibition game Dormont started off with Fest and the Grays with Joe Strong. Eventually Joe Semler came in for Dormont and Arnold Waites and Willie Gesentaner for the

Grays as both teams tried to stop the others hitting in an 11-7 Dormont win.

Semi-pro baseball in Pittsburgh seems to have taken a backseat to the minor and major league game summaries from its hay day in the 20's and early 30's. Sports writers weren't giving it much attention and the box scores were really basic and not as detailed like they used to be. Take for example that last game with Dormont and the Grays. I wrote more about the game than the newspaper did. I think this shows the shift in baseball culture and the decline and lack of interest in semi-pro baseball.

Getting his first official start with Dormont Joe took the mound against Immaculate Heart on the 8th at Dormont. They were up 6-3 when Joe was relieved by Malloy who took it the rest of the way for a 12-4 win.

Dormont cruised to 1st place in the city league after Joe handed the Homestead Merchants a 20-7 beating on the 15th of July. The win gave them a record of 4-0.

By the 23rd the Wilkes-Barre papers were reporting that Joe might be coming back to play for the Barons. Jake Pitler says he has made him an enticing offer to get him back. The Barons were currently in 5th place with a record of 10-10 and could use some help.

It only took Joe a day to decide to accept the offer and the Wilkes-Barre papers were abuzz about his return. Jake Pitler said *"I'm tickled to death to have Semler back. I think he is a good pitcher and will give the club the needed assistance in the hurling division. He has the experience and plenty of stuff on the ball yet. Just watch our smoke now.*"[46]

Joe returned on the 27th of July to face Hazleton in front of 750 Baron fans. Going against Hughie Mulcahy Joe struck out the first 2 batters he faced. But after that the Mountaineers were ahead 6-0 before the Barons finally scored a run in the bottom of the 6th inning to make it 6-1. The final was a 7-3 loss for Joe and sent the Barons back to 6th place. Mulcahy would go on to win 25 games for Hazleton this year and pitched 323 innings which set a league record.

Traveling on the 1st of August Joe got the start against the Senators in Trenton, New Jersey. After the 1st half of the season York dropped out of the league and the Trenton, New Jersey Senators joined the league. Joe pitched a nice game and with plenty of bat support got an 8-7 win. The win made Joe 5-4 with the Barons this season.

Back in Wilkes-Barre on the 11th Joe got his next start against Atley Donald and the Triplets. The Barons scored their only run in the 1st inning and after that it was all in favor of the Triplets. They scored 6 runs to take away a 6-1 win. It wasn't the best day for Joe to have a bad day because the scout for the Pittsburgh Pirates was in the stands watching the game.

Getting the start against Trenton in the early game of a double header on the 15th Joe took the mound in front of 1,000 fans. He was on his game and held the Senators hitless for 7 innings and only allowed 3 hits in the game. He threw 4 strikeouts in an impressive 7-0 shutout. Now this is the game the Pirate scout should have been at! Johnny Day started the night cap but he was relieved by tobacco chewing Ace Elliott who got the 4-3 win and sweep.

Playing Elmira on the 20th Joe took the mound against Lew Krausse at Dunn Field. The game went back and forth and was tied 1-1 in the 4th inning and 3-3 in the 7th inning. Then in the bottom of the 8th inning Joe gave up 4 runs to make it 7-3. The Barons scored 2 more runs in the top of the 9th but it wasn't enough and lost 7-5. It was the 19th win for Lew Krausse and he would go on to win 24 games for Elmira this season.

It was a trip to Hazleton for a double header at Buhler Stadium on the 23rd. Ace Elliott got the start and was in big trouble losing 10-1 after 6 innings. Joe came in relief but there wasn't much he could do at that point. He gave up another run in an 11-1 beating. Johnny Day pitched the night cap in a nicely won 2-1 game. The Barons were in 6th place with a record of 22-26.

Playing the Mountaineers on the 25th in Hazleton Joe got the start and a win in probably the weirdest game he ever played. Hazleton was up 2-0 going into the top of the 7th inning. Joe got a single. Then Hubie Fitzgerald singled into right field and the right fielder threw the ball to the 3rd baseman in an attempt to get Joe who was trying to make it to 3rd base. The ball took a high hop in front of the 3rd baseman and went over his head. Joe kept going and scored. At the end of 7 innings the Mountaineers were leading 3-1. In the top of the 8th inning the

Barons scored 4 runs to take the lead 4-3. About that time a huge storm was starting to move in. Hazleton started to stall the game hoping it would get called due to rain and revert back to the last full inning, in which they were winning. But after stalling for 23 minutes and listening to Jake Pitler scream bloody murder the umpire called the game in favor of the Barons and Joe got a 4-3 win!

Hosting Williamsport in a double header on the 30th Joe took the early game in front of 2,000 hometown fans. Going against Ed Smith Joe pitched a nice game keeping the Grays hits scattered in a 5-3 win. Charlie Willis took the night cap and pitched a close 10 inning game that went for a 3-2 loss.

Allentown came to Wilkes-Barre on the 3rd of September and Joe went up against Bob Barr. It was a nice tight game and Joe was ahead 4-3 going into the top of the 7th inning. Then the Brooks opened up on him for a triple, 2 doubles, and a pair of singles scoring 4 runs. A couple of fielding errors by his teammates didn't help. Charlie Willis came in relief but the damage was done and the Barons lost 7-5. The Barons had 6 fielding errors in the game to include the shortstop and the 2nd baseman both not touching 2nd base on force plays. The things that make a pitcher pull his hair out….

Elmer Yoter brought his Scranton Miners to Wilkes-Barre for a double header on Labor Day and 1,100 fans came out under a cloudy sky. Dutch Schessler started the early game, but more Baron errors and lethargic playing led to a 7-2 Miner win. Joe took the night cap against Milt Shoffner and lost it 4-2. It was Milt's 18th win of the season and his 10th in the past 11 games.

It was a fitting way for Joe to end the 1936 season when the Barons took on the Brooks in Allentown on the 12th of September. Taking the mound against Wally Signor Joe pitched a nice game only giving up runs towards the later innings and won it 9-6.

Wilkes-Barre came in 6th place with a record of 30-38 for the 2nd half of the season. Joe finished up with a record of 9-8, Charlie Willis was 17-17, Ace Elliott was 7-6, and Johnny Day was 9-10.

The Scranton Miners who won the 1st half of the season took on the Elmira Pioneers, the 2nd half winners, for the 1936 NYP League Championship title. Elmer Yoter's Miners won it in 5 games.

The Late Years
1937 to 1940's

1937:

It was assumed that Joe would be back with the Barons for the 1937 season. But as spring training arrived he hadn't shown up and the papers were saying that he was holding out, which wasn't unusual for Joe. Every year he seemed to be one of the last ones to negotiate a deal and sign his contract. But as the last days of spring training were winding down without him he surprisingly asked the league to retire him, which they did. Joe was quoted in the papers as saying he wanted to stay in McKees Rocks and devote more time to the family construction business.

He did have four kids to look after and he had recently remarried, so I think he was wanting to spend more time at home. And it seemed like his arm had been giving him more and more trouble.

But in September the papers were reporting that Joe had asked to come out of retirement but the league denied his request. I'm not sure what could have precipitated this request. Maybe after sitting out his first baseball season in 17 years he realized he missed it. And there was the financial aspect of not playing, he might have missed that income.

1938:

Joe had dabbled with getting back into baseball, or at least keeping himself busy over the summer and joined the Stowe team in Pittsburgh's City League. Although I don't think he pitched any games with them, at least they didn't make the papers.

He did participate in a game at Forbes Field on August 7th celebrating the 25th anniversary of the Homestead Grays. A crowd of 5,000 came out to see the All-Stars take on the Ex-Grays and it was a who's who of semi-pro baseball players of the 20's & early 30's. For the All-Stars there was Carl Stewart, Joe and Jim Swetonic, Art Shaw, Jack Ripper, Eddie Artman, Jack Miller, Skipper Douds, Gene Malarkey, Art Schell, Ed Ludwig, Bill Fuchs, Abe Martin, Bill Rittleman, Rhiney Kress, and Joe Semler. For the Ex-Grays there was "Smokey" Joe Williams, Lefty Williams, Willis Moody, Moe Harris, Sam Streeter, Oscar Owens, Harry Solman, Dennis Graham, Buddy Carpenter, Laudie Walker, Sell Hall, "Rags" Roberts, and Jasper Washington.

The game was far from just a get together and the veteran ball players showed their skill. The Ex-Grays won it 5-2. After the game the Negro National League held a game between the Homestead Grays and Newark Eagles. The Grays won 8-4.

The picture below is from the All-Stars and Ex-Grays game.

—Post-Gazette Photo.

A galaxy of baseball stars from yesteryear performed at Forbes Field yesterday as the Homestead Grays celebrated their twenty-fifth anniversary. Two teams of old-timers, one representing the Grays and the other their opponents of long ago, played before a large crowd. The picture shows, front row, left to right, Carl Stewart, Joe Swetonic, Art Shaw, Jack Ripper. Second row, Eddie Artman, Jack Miller, Skipper Douds, Gene Malarkey, Art Schell. Back row, Ed Ludwig, and Joe Semler. The former Grays won the game 5 to 2.

All-Stars against the Ex-Grays 1938[43]

My dad asked Joe in the late 70's about pitching against the Homestead Grays and he said *"I could pretty near break-even with em' Ed. But if a fella beat them once in a life time he was doing pretty good."*[47] He went on to say that he figured he won 8 games against them. Well Joe was spot on in his recollection of his past games with the Grays. I figured in his lifetime he was 8-11 against them with 1 tie.

1939:

On the 20th of July Joe got into another old timers game when the Dormont Old Timers took on the Dormont Dukes at Dormont High Field. The Old Timers included Wilbur Cooper, Charlie Thomas, Gene Malarkey, George Striker, Beggs Snyder, Abe Martin, and Joe Semler. I couldn't find a game summary for this but it must have gotten the pitching juices flowing with Joe because he went on to play a few games for the minor league Johnstown Johnnies in August.

The Johnnies were a Class-D minor league team in the Pennsylvania State Association and a farm team for the major league Philadelphia Phillies.

On the 23rd of August he took the mound against the Butler Yankees in Butler and held them to 5 hits in a 4-2 win. It turns out that he was pitching at the request of his good friend Dick Goldberg who was managing the Johnnies.

He got in one more game before the season ended on the 27th when Johnstown hosted Butler. He pitched a 7-6 game and went all 9 innings. He also had 3 hits in the game and drove in 2 runs. Not bad for 39 years old.

In September Joe was asked to play on a team of All-Stars being put together by Ottie Cochran to play a team of inmates from the Western Penitentiary on the 23rd of August. Joe played along with Wilber Cooper, Skinny Wright, Wago Anthony, Dan Taylor, Jack Cummings, John Zeglot, Leo Carroll and Al Lucas. Joe shared in the pitching duties and the All-Stars won 9-4.

1940:

Once again Joe was asked to play on Ottie Cochran's All-Star team against the Western Penitentiary on the 27th of July. The team consisted of Harry Fowler, Jim Mitchell, Dan Daugherty, Ed Kelly, Jack Cummings, Vic Steigerwald, Steve Adley, Joe & Cook Hadley, Ray Bond, Tom Carson, Joe Gruber, Al Lucas Leo Carroll, Chuck Meider, and Billy Fuchs. Joe and Leo Carroll were said to have pitched a great game in another 9-4 win.

1941:

Joe played on an Old Timers team put together to play a team from Crafton-Ingram at Crafton High Field on the 16th of July. The proceeds of the game would benefit the Greater Pittsburgh Amateur Baseball Federation. The team was a great reunion of the old Homewood and Beaver Fall Elks players Joe played with back in the late 20's and consisted of Elmer Knetzer, Bimmy Steele, Heinie Boll, Wago Anthony, Elmer Wyssier, Al Dunn, Dick Cooley, Harry Fowler, Gummy Snellbacher, Billy Fuchs, Stan Berkman, Jack Cummings, Leo Carroll, Dave

Wickline and Joe's brother Al "Curly" Semler. Crafton won the game 9-5.

1942:

Once again the Old Timers got together to play Bethany College on the 13th of May at Crafton High Field in a game to benefit the Greater Pittsburgh Baseball Federation. The game drew 300 fans and had pretty much the same lineup as last year. The Old Timers shut out the college boys 6-0!

The picture below is of the pre-game chatter and Leo Carroll is showing how he gripped the ball when he threw his "splitter."

BIMMY STEELE   JOE SEMLER   GEO. McFARLAND   LEO CARROLL   HERB HURST

Old Timers against Bethany College 1942[44]

Getting asked to play on Ottie Cochran's All-Star team again they played the Corbins on the 24th of June at the New Kensington High Stadium. The game was to benefit the Greater Pittsburgh Baseball Federation.

And on the 27th he was on a team of veteran ball players in a benefit game against the Fifteenth Ward Service League. The benefits going to boys joining military service. He played on several of these teams throughout the war supporting programs that helped men who were joining the service and going off to fight in World War II.

Joe went on to play on many teams throughout the 1940's that pitted veteran ball players against local teams to raise money for various charities and organizations. It was his way of staying active in the baseball community and helping out in the Pittsburgh area.

He was lucky enough to have played baseball as a premier player for so many years and became well known in the greater Pittsburgh area. And I think that's why his baseball story is so interesting, because it covered such a large part of baseball as it came of age in America. Sure, his story is limited to Pennsylvania in many respects but its representative of all of baseball in America during that time period. When baseball at all levels, not just the major leagues, was a vibrant national past time.

Joe was a devoutly religious man who never missed Sunday Mass and prayed the Rosary every day. I know he would want me to end this book with a hearty

"God Bless"

Minor League Stats

Year	Team	W – L	ERA
1931	Hazleton Mountaineers	12 -17	4.08
1932	Hazleton Mountaineers	4 - 7	
1932	Scranton Miners	0 - 0	
1932	York White Roses	3 – 3	
1932	Combined three teams	7 -10	5.92
1933	Wilkes-Barre Barons	13 – 4	2.32
1934	Wilkes-Barre Barons	20 -12	3.20
1935	Nashville Volunteers	0 – 2	4.97
1935	Wilkes-Barre Barons	12 – 8	4.75
1936	Wilkes-Barre Barons	9 – 8	4.50

Resources

1. Pittsburgh Post-Gazette 24 December 1969 article by Andy Dugo

2. Pittsburgh Post-Gazette 3 December 1969 article by Andy Dugo

3. Pittsburgh Press page 22, 22 June 1919

4. Brooklineconnection.com

5. Semler Family archives

6. Pittsburgh Press page 23, 11 May 1921

7. Pittsburgh Daily Post page 32, 24 June 1923

8. Pittsburgh Daily Post page 36, 20 April 1924

9. Pittsburgh Post-Gazette 9 September 1923

10. Pittsburgh Daily Post page 35, 8 June 1924

11. Pittsburgh Daily Post page 28, 14 September 1924

12. Pittsburgh Post-Gazette page 14, 23 May 1925

13. Pittsburgh Daily Post page 29, 7 June 1925

14. Pittsburgh Daily Post page 21, 5 July 1925

15. Pittsburgh Post-Gazette page 13, 14 July 1925

16. Pittsburgh Post-Gazette 18 September 1925

17. Pittsburgh Post-Gazette page 16, 14 April 1926

18. Pittsburgh Daily Post page 29, 1 August 1926

19. Pittsburgh Press page 20, 31 Aug 1919

20. Pittsburgh Press page 26, 24 Aug 1919

21. Pittsburgh Press page 26, 6 October 1926

22. Pittsburgh Daily Post page 24, 17 July 1927

23 Pittsburgh Press page 47, 21 August 1927

24. Pittsburgh Press page 46, 26 August 1928

25. Pittsburgh Press page 12, 29 June 1929

26. Pittsburgh Post-Gazette page 19, 18 June 1929

27. Pittsburgh Press page 45, 2 September 1929

28. Pittsburgh Sun-Telegraph page 23, 25 May 1930

29. Pittsburgh Press page 26, 8 July 1930

30. Standard-Speaker page 17, 26 June 1931

31. Pittsburgh Press page 30, 15 March 1932

32. The Plain Speaker page 10, 11 April 1932

33. The Plain Speaker page 20, 15 July 1932

34. Pittsburgh Sun-Telegraph page 24, 14 June 1933

35. The Plain Speaker page 8, 17 June 1933

36. The Evening News page 16, 1 May 1934

37. The Wilkes-Barre Record page 15, 10 July 1934

38. The Plain Speaker page 21, 7 September 1934

39. Nashville Banner page 8, 18 March 1935

40. Nashville Banner page 14, 21 March 1935

41. Nashville Banner page 8, 26 March 1935

42. The Tennessean 19 May 1935

43. Pittsburgh Post-Gazette page14, 8 August 1938

44. Pittsburgh Post-Gazette page 17, 14 May 1942

45. Wilkes-Barre Record page 20, 10 June 1936

46. Wilkes-Barre Record page 18, 24 July 1936

47. Tape of Ed Semler interviewing Joe Semler in the late 70's

48. Cincinnati Enquirer page 72, 24 September 1922

About the Author

Ed Semler retired from the United States Coast Guard in December of 2007 with over 25 years of military service in both the United States Army and United States Coast Guard. In the United States Army he was an enlisted man and was honorably discharged as a Specialist Four (E-4). While in the United States Coast Guard he was enlisted, obtaining the rank of Master Chief Petty Officer (E-9), was commissioned as an officer, and retired as a Lieutenant (O-3E).

After his military career Ed dabbled in teaching at a Vocational Technical School and was a self-employed plumber for several years. As a past time he enjoys writing and playing the guitar, bass, piano, bugle and harmonica.

Fully retired he resides in Schulenburg, Texas with his wife Jana, a retired Air Force senior master sergeant. Please feel free to check out Ed's other books at www.edsemler.com or email him at mkcm378@gmail.com

His other publications are;

"Around The World," a memoir of his 25 years of service as an officer and enlisted man in the U.S. Army and U.S. Coast Guard

"U.S. Coast Guard Cutter Sherman (WHEC-720) Circumnavigation Deployment 2001" which details the *Sherman's* historic circumnavigation of the globe and deployment to the Persian Gulf in 2001

"The Three Gunsallus Brothers" a story about fighting for Pennsylvania during the Civil War

"Sam Houston & Napoleon Bonaparte Meet On The Civil War Battlefield" a true story of the Walker brothers

"Thoughts On Being A Chief Petty Officer" a take on military leadership

"Fighting For Pennsylvania In The Early Years 1763 to 1783 – The Story of Captain Thomas Askey And Lieutenant Richard Gunsalus Of Cumberland County"

www.ingramcontent.com/pod-product-compliance
Lightning Source LLC
LaVergne TN
LVHW051359080426
835508LV00022B/2901